Also by Diana Kapp

Girls Who Run the World: 31 CEOs Who Mean Business

GIRLS WHO GREEN THE WORLD

THIRTY-FOUR REBEL WOMEN OUT TO SAVE OUR PLANET

Diana Kapp
Illustrated by Ana Jarén

Delacorte Press

Visit us on the Web! GetUnderlined.com

Educators and librarians, for a variety of teaching tools, visit us at
RHTeachersLibrarians.com

Library of Congress Cataloging-in-Publication Data
Names: Kapp, Diana, author. | Jarén, Ana, illustrator.
Title: Girls who green the world : 34 rebel women out to save our planet /
Diana Kapp ; Illustrated by Ana Jarén.
Description: First edition. | New York : Delacorte Press, [2022] | Audience: Ages
14 and up | Summary: "A guidebook to the modern environmental movement
featuring 34 inspiring women working to save our planet"—Provided by publisher.
Identifiers: LCCN 2021018703 (print) | LCCN 2021018704 (ebook) |
ISBN 978-0-593-42805-4 (hardcover) | ISBN 978-0-593-48434-0 (library binding) |
ISBN 978-0-593-42806-1 (ebook)
Subjects: LCSH: Women environmentalists—Juvenile literature. | Women and the
environment—Juvenile literature. | Environmental protection—Juvenile literature.
Classification: LCC GE195.9 .K37 2022 (print) | LCC GE195.9 (ebook) |
DDC 333.72092/52 [B]—dc23

The text of this book is set in 10-point Gotham.
Interior design by Andrea Lau

Printed in Italy
10 9 8 7 6 5 4 3 2 1
First Edition

For my kids and their kids, because there is no planet B.
And for so many young people out there
who are struggling to find hope.

CONTENTS

INTRODUCTION

You might remember learning about a terrifying hole in the atmosphere that nearly did us in back in the 1980s. Or maybe you've never even heard about it. Nowadays, educators often skip the topic altogether because that ozone hole is filed away under "problem solved." But back when the hole was at its largest, scientists were really freaking out. Without an intact atmospheric layer acting like a giant beach umbrella blocking the sun's radiation, we were all gonna fry, they said.

The panic high point was around 1986. An emergency meeting was convened in Boulder, Colorado. Scientists gathered from all over. The leaders of the conference sought a volunteer to head up a mission to the South Pole—where the hole was most pronounced—to study the phenomenon. For an uncomfortable second, no one volunteered. Then Susan Solomon, a young computational chemist who spent her days creating complex atmospheric models, raised her hand. She wasn't really a fieldwork scientist, but she knew her way around a spectrograph, which would be the critical instrument for the South Pole research. "I'll go," she blurted.

The reaction from the crowd—a dismissive shrug followed by titters—was not unfamiliar. Earlier that day, she'd presented her novel theory on why the ozone hole had opened in the first place, but no one had seemed particularly convinced or impressed then, either.

She'd based the theory on a decades-old study of chlorofluorocarbons (CFCs), chemicals found in things like refrigerants, hair spray, and aerosol deodorant. The study had warned that CFCs could very slowly destroy the ozone layer. Susan had zeroed in on chemical reactions to answer two questions: If CFCs were used widely, why was the ozone hole appearing only in the spring and summer? And why was the hole centered over Antarctica? She pinpointed the exact altitude of maximum loss and recognized that the preponderance of clouds was a clue.

Susan posited that there were two things helping CFCs destroy the ozone layer. For the necessary chemical reactions to happen, the CFCs needed sunlight to break the chemical compounds apart, since UV radiation is one of the few things that can undo those molecules' bonds. They also needed something to sit on . . . like nice tiny ice crystals in all those gathering polar clouds she'd noticed. Susan hypothesized that in these perfect conditions, CFCs were breaking apart and releasing chlorine, which was destroying the ozone, which then released more chlorine, in an ever-accelerating, terrifying loop.

It was ridiculous to her audience, all men. And the bit about the clouds—that was practically "heretical," as Susan recounted. And now this woman with the crackpot theory wanted to lead the expedition to the South Pole?

Well, yes. And four months later, she did, and touched down in Antarctica with sixteen thousand pounds of equipment and her team of fifteen. She worked eighteen-hour days, often perched atop a building in temps below -40 degrees, angling her mirror to direct light through a hole they'd cut in the roof, and then through a prism in the spectrograph. The colors produced indicated how strongly wavelengths of light were being absorbed, which revealed the concentration of chlorine.

Her finding: the presence of chlorine dioxide a hundred times normal levels. And the ever-accelerating loop she'd discovered—the destruction was anything but slow. Earth was facing a ticking time bomb. When this news hit the front pages, the world jumped. The United Nations convened a summit in Montreal. Given the findings and theory, every developed country swore off CFC production immediately, and the rest of the world soon followed. The Montreal Protocol remains a singular case of every nation on earth linking arms to avert an environmental cataclysm.

Ever since, the hole has been closing. It's the greatest environmental turnaround to date.

Right now, we need Susan's story more than ever. Certainly other environmental trailblazers have left their indelible mark—Rachel Carson, with *Silent Spring,* sounding the alarm on the evils of man-made chemicals like DDT. Eunice Newton Foote, in 1856, publishing the very first words on the warming capability of carbon dioxide—"an atmosphere of that gas would give to our earth a high temperature." But Susan Solomon embodies notions that are utterly fundamental—that government action works; that following the science works; and, presciently, that even dire environmental catastrophe can be headed off.

These are urgent times. You don't need a litany of horror-inducing facts—like that all Americans combined drive the equivalent of five hundred round trips from Earth to Pluto each year, or that Coca-Cola churns out two hundred thousand plastic bottles a minute. The fact that we have eight years to cut greenhouse gases in half in order to avert . . . well, mass extinction, is old news. You've heard that women are particularly vulnerable, facing assault and domestic violence at higher rates when there are climate-related disasters or environmental destruction. You can spew all of this in your sleep.

You have never known a day without climate emergency. Eco-anxiety is your constant. And you know, like you know water is wet, that the worst trap is defeatist thinking, cynicism, or complacency. A loud chorus says we're running out of time. . . . It's probably too late already. . . . I'm only one person . . . and what difference can one person make?

Girls Who Green the World is about fighters who have no patience for any of that doubt. It's a magic doorway into an alternate universe of possibility, buzzing and whirring with mad scientists and doers, every single one racing impatiently to head off planetary disaster.

In these pages are thirty-four intrepid change-makers who choose possibility. They refuse to be cowed by a ticking clock. I could have included 234 more women. That's because there's a revolution happening, and there are hundreds and thousands of revolutionaries to admire.

They are turning exhaled breath into chicken, mushrooms into leather, and plastic bottles into boardshorts that turn into car-seat stuffing. They are hell-bent on reviving our oceans, heating homes with carbon-neutral geothermal energy, and dyeing jeans with bioengineered indigo that doesn't turn rivers in China black.

This new guard is breaking from the environmental movement's problematic roots. They are facing down the grave injustices to Native people and lands, reckoning with the outsized burdens of pollution and chemical exposure thrust on marginalized communities, insisting on environmental justice. They recognize clean air and water as human rights.

Some of the advances are half measures, a change in mindset on the way toward becoming a change in paradigm. Biodegradable glitter. Ugly pickles, made from misshapen cukes that would otherwise be tossed. These initiatives matter as much as the biggies. Sure, chips made of the pulp from juicing machines won't instantly lower the methane meter, but when their creator, Kaitlin Mogentale, expands Pulp Pantry into an empire, upcycling billions of pounds of byproduct into cereal, pie crusts, pasta, tortillas, flour . . . that is how we start to change the entire industrial food complex.

These trailblazers make cool heroes—they are highly trained chemical engineers and theoretical high-energy physicists, contrarian biologists and agriculture scientists, deft marketers and business mavericks. They are selling the world on solar, planting carbon-sequestering (and tasty) sea vegetables, and cleaning toxins out of water, backyards, and cosmetics. One blocked the Dakota Access Pipeline with the weight of her body. They are making waves as agitators, policy wonks, culture shifters, and inventors. Oh, and they are all women.

Despite their brilliance and cunning, recognition for these women is still too rare. They receive too little funding and not enough ink.

Most of the women you'll read about here are young. Young people have always driven social change. Ruby Bridges was just six when she walked her bobby-socked feet up the steps of William Frantz Elementary School, where all the students were white, and she became the first Black student there. Emma González was a high schooler when she woke the world up to gun madness. The Vietnam War was brought down by young people. And Greta Thunberg. Greta! In 2018 she was a lone schoolgirl sitting outside Sweden's Parliament, demanding attention. The next year she had 1.6 million schoolkids in thirty countries taking climate change ultimatums to the streets.

Rhiana Gunn-Wright, age thirty-three, was inspired by these young activists. It's girls like Ruby and Greta that Rhiana was thinking about when she put pen to paper and sketched the tenets of the Green New Deal. The plan creates new jobs, new industries even, and curbs airline and car pollution. It insists on equity, and turns upside down practically everything we know about industry and government. Some have called it impossible. Others have ridiculed it.

Not the girls inheriting this planet.

On the morning after the 2021 inauguration, a dozen youth activists, all but one of them girls, posted an open letter to President Biden and Vice President Harris. Biden's stated goal of achieving net-zero emissions by 2050 is simply too late. "Be braver," they wrote. "People are burning, drowning, and dying. Enough," the young environmentalists implored.

Biden heard. He revised his targets, lopping off fifteen years to achieve a carbon-free power sector by 2035.

You have power. Presidents are listening to you. Just cracking open this book, you have set off a cultural chain reaction that cannot stop. These thirty-four trailblazers, they are links in that chain, too. Susan Solomon and her ozone discovery, she was a link in that chain, too, as women have always been and will continue to be on the front lines of this movement. Instead of being fueled by a universal CFC ban, this transformation is fueled by insistence and persistence. By a sense of possibility. By hope. Theirs and yours.

Author's Note: I interviewed each of the thirty-four women profiled. You can assume that all unattributed quotes come from my personal interviews with them. If there was another source, I indicate that.

How We Got Here

To walk ourselves away from this climate ledge, we need to understand how we got here.

Why is the earth warming so much, so quickly?

It's all, quite simply, a matter of chemistry.

The story starts with the Industrial Revolution. In the late 1700s, in Britain, society started modernizing. Farmers and businesspeople wanted to produce more with less sweat. They had used up the available wood for cooking and warming their homes, so needed a new energy source. The early industrialists discovered that they had easy access to mine stores of coal, a rock buried deep in the earth that when burned produces energy. Because coal burned so well, these Brits developed the coal-powered steam engine, which mechanized cotton gins and enabled steel mills. Soon, factories were constructed with growing assembly lines, then steamships and, ultimately, railroads.

Productivity soared because merchants could now sell their goods far and wide, import new raw materials, and make many copies of a product all at once, cheaply and quickly. This efficient way of producing things spread to America. Electricity was invented, then the automobile and the airplane, all run on fossil fuels. Lives were improving because people had better-paying jobs, heat, transportation, tools that simplified work. All of this drove further innovation. Modernization built on coal spread around the world, spurring the growth of cities, an explosion in commerce, and a booming population.

In the mid-1700s, the earth's population was around 760 million. That number has now ballooned to 7.6 billion people. But what makes such growth a hazard of epic proportions is the quantity of fossil fuel being burned to support all these people. In roughly the same period of time, worldwide fossil fuel use has exploded 1,400 times.

Then we decided to ignore the problem. As far back as the 1850s, scientists were noting the heat-trapping property of carbon dioxide (a gas emitted during all that fossil fuel burning). Climate science pioneer Eunice Foote—yes, a woman!—compared the temperature of various gases she trapped in glass cylinders, presciently reporting "an atmosphere of that gas [carbon dioxide] would give to our earth a high temperature" in a paper presented before the American Association for the Advancement of Science. And scientist John Tyndall even linked this property of carbon dioxide to climate change. But society did not heed these early warnings. We were too busy extracting and burning fuel, growing our economies, consuming, and continuously upgrading. The instinct to expand makes sense, and did plenty of good, but we've gone way overboard.

Did you know that coal, as well as oil and gas, are called fossil fuels because they are literally fossils? They are plants, and dinosaurs, and dead trees and fish, left to rot hundreds of millions of years ago. Coal specifically formed from huge dead trees from the Carboniferous period, some three hundred million years ago when the earth was swampy. The trees got covered with water, then sediment, and underground, with immense pressure and heat, they became part of the earth's crust. Shale, a type of rock that releases oil, started as algae, crustaceans, and plants fossilized in mud. Petroleum is mostly dead plankton and sea plants from the bottoms of once-oceans.

What's so wrong with burning millions of tons of fossils? To understand, we need to talk basic science for a sec. The plants, the polar bears, the fish, we humans are all made of carbon. Carbon is an element, the basic building block of living things, and when carbon is burned, or combusted, or metabolized, or breathed out, carbon dioxide (CO_2) gets emitted.

Plants suck carbon dioxide in through their leaves and, using the sun's energy, convert it into food, which is how they grow buds or thick trunks. When humans or animals eat plants, they "burn" carbon for fuel, and exhale carbon dioxide. All the dead plants and animals that aren't consumed—"the little bit left in the corner of the sardine can that you can't get out," as a 2020 *Economist* piece put it—get stored deep underground and ultimately become fossil fuels and, when mined and burned, emit carbon dioxide. The ocean absorbs one-third of all the earth's carbon dioxide to sustain plant and fish life, and also releases carbon dioxide back into the air. The oceans, because they absorb so much carbon dioxide, and take in more when there is excess in the atmosphere, have acted as a buffer, keeping Earth's CO_2 levels in check.

For 800,000 years, carbon dioxide quantities in the atmosphere shifted constantly, but still stayed within a narrow range—between 175 and 280 parts per million (ppm). Even through multiple ice ages and warm eras, atmospheric carbon dioxide didn't budge above 320 ppm, according to National Oceanic and Atmospheric Administration (NOAA) data. Steady eddy.

But around 1950, graphs of carbon dioxide levels started making like a hockey stick and curving up quickly, showing that carbon dioxide was deviating from its stable past. Today, carbon dioxide in the earth's atmosphere measures 415 ppm. What is most alarming is the rate of growth. In just the past seventy years, atmospheric carbon dioxide has increased over 100 percent. The dire issue is the heat-trapping property of carbon dioxide (acting a bit like a greenhouse, which is why we say "greenhouse gases") that Eunice Foote recognized, because CO_2 hangs around for a very long time, building up and building up, and trapping ever more heat.

In a nutshell: millions of years' worth of fossilized plants and animals were underground emitting no CO_2, and in a nanosecond—in geological time—we have transferred a gargantuan amount of carbon from being sequestered and inert to filling the atmosphere with heat-trapping greenhouse gases. Seventy-five percent of global greenhouse gas emissions are caused by our burning fossil fuels, according to the Intergovernmental Panel on Climate Change (IPCC). Then, piling on methane, another greenhouse gas—emitted by food in landfills; and by the cows for all our burgers, belching and farting; and from limestone when made into cement—has been building up. Methane is a super trapper, holding heat thirty times more effectively than CO_2. Our burning down rain forests to grow crops, leading to fewer trees that are absorbing CO_2, has turned the sauna up even more. The heat is warming the oceans, making it harder for the ocean to act as a buffer for our increased emissions, because warmer waters can't absorb as much carbon dioxide. The heat also thaws permafrost soil, which allows more stored carbon dioxide and methane out into the atmosphere. So, you see, planet

How We Got Here

Earth is a big interconnected system, hurling with more and more velocity in a terrifying direction.

The rate of change is what makes the current warming trajectory so dangerous. With our industrial economy every year transferring 9.5 billion tons of fossil fuels out of the earth and into the atmosphere, according to the NOAA, we're causing drastic changes to Earth on a time scale so fast that life cannot adapt. We are seeing that humans now have a power over Earth as great as, or greater than, the forces of nature. (There's even a term for the epoch marked by this being the case—the Anthropocene.)

We are seeing that humans now have a power over Earth as great as, or greater than, the forces of nature.

Global warming, too, is far from the only planetary devastation that we humans are driving. According to research done by the University of Georgia and the University of California, our throwaway-plastic culture has produced a global mass of plastic equivalent in weight to 80 million blue whales, or 822,000 Eiffel Towers, or one billion elephants—pick your favorite comparison—most of which is now sitting in landfills. Chemical runoff from producing the clothing to keep pace with our ever faster, trend-chasing fashion cycles are turning the world's waterways toxic. Add to these hazards the pollutant-spewing factories, most situated in poor and minority areas, that cause disproportionate rates of cancer, asthma, and lung disease relative to rates in more affluent communities.

But global warming is our dire emergency. As the buildup of greenhouse gases leads to more and more warming, we get a whole host of other problems that we are already seeing increasingly cause destruction, displacement, and death: rising sea levels, immense wildfires, extreme storms. And the most vulnerable among us suffer from the effects most intensely.

In 2018, the IPCC issued its Special Report on Global Warming of 1.5 C, calling for a 45 percent reduction in fossil fuel emissions from 2010 levels by 2030, and for achieving net-zero emissions by 2050. The urgency is an attempt to keep the global temperature increase, compared to pre-industrial times, well below 2°C. But keeping our global warming below that number will be incredibly challenging. We are now in completely un-charted territory.

This is why we must stop burning fossil fuels—yesterday. Government policies like taxing or capping emissions levels, and financial incentives for instituting carbon-cutting, have a critical role to play. We need to keep operationalizing solar and wind power, and devise ways to store that clean power. We have to invent fuels that don't emit carbon dioxide, and tech-nologies to take out and lock away carbon dioxide that's already hang-ing around. We need to breed fewer cows; protect rain forests; plant kelp and mangroves, which sequester carbon dioxide and stabilize shorelines; stem ocean acidification caused by an oversupply of carbon dioxide in the water, before we destroy all our underwater habitats. We need to use every cell of creative brainpower to do away with coal, oil, and gas and meet our needs other ways, and replace the practices destroying people and the planet with even craftier solutions that allow all of us to meet our potential.

These women are how we get there from here.

HOW WE GOT HERE

The only way to reverse global warming and environmental destruction is to first have an honest reckoning with how we got into this mess. This "map" represents many of the key drivers. Note the many hockey-stick-shaped graphs going steeply up and right.

FOSSIL FUEL
fuels climate change

The burning of fossil fuel is the single largest source of global temperature rise.[1]

Burning coal is responsible for 44% of CO_2 emissions worldwide.[4]

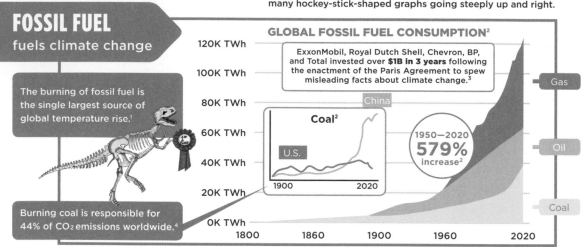

GLOBAL FOSSIL FUEL CONSUMPTION[2]

ExxonMobil, Royal Dutch Shell, Chevron, BP, and Total invested over **$1B in 3 years** following the enactment of the Paris Agreement to spew misleading facts about climate change.[3]

Coal[2]

China

U.S.

1900   2020

1950—2020
579%
increase[2]

Gas

Oil

Coal

120K TWh
100K TWh
80K TWh
60K TWh
40K TWh
20K TWh
0K TWh

1800   1860   1900   1960   2020

CARS
driving up the heat

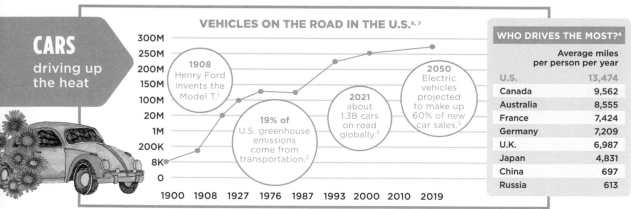

VEHICLES ON THE ROAD IN THE U.S.[5,7]

1908 Henry Ford invents the Model T.[1]

19% of U.S. greenhouse emissions come from transportation.[2]

2021 about 1.3B cars on road globally.[3]

2050 Electric vehicles projected to make up 60% of new car sales.[5]

300M
250M
200M
150M
100M
20M
1M
200K
8K
0

1900 1908 1927 1976 1987 1993 2000 2010 2019

WHO DRIVES THE MOST?[4]

	Average miles per person per year
U.S.	13,474
Canada	9,562
Australia	8,555
France	7,424
Germany	7,209
U.K.	6,987
Japan	4,831
China	697
Russia	613

PLASTIC
is forever

Plastic was found in 98% of soil samples taken in 11 U.S. National Parks.[1]

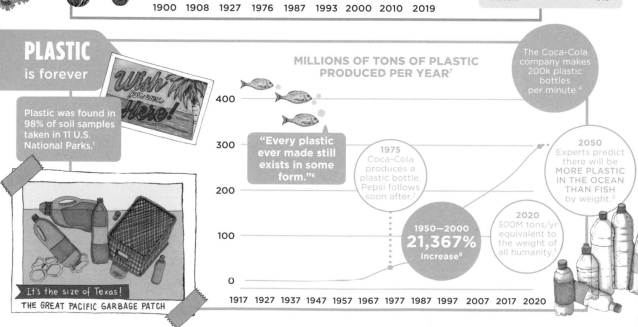

It's the size of Texas!
THE GREAT PACIFIC GARBAGE PATCH

MILLIONS OF TONS OF PLASTIC PRODUCED PER YEAR[7]

The Coca-Cola company makes 200k plastic bottles per minute.[4]

"Every plastic ever made still exists in some form."[6]

1975 Coca-Cola produces a plastic bottle. Pepsi follows soon after.[2]

1950—2000
21,367%
increase[8]

2020 300M tons/yr equivalent to the weight of all humanity.[5]

2050 Experts predict there will be MORE PLASTIC IN THE OCEAN THAN FISH by weight.[3]

400

300

200

100

0

1917 1927 1937 1947 1957 1967 1977 1987 1997 2007 2017 2020

FAST FASHION
throwaway culture defined

10% of global greenhouse emissions come from fashion.[1]

Every time we wash a synthetic garment **ABOUT 1,900 INDIVIDUAL MICROFIBERS** are released into the water to make their way into our oceans.[2]

Plastic in clothes is one of the leading contributors to ocean plastic.

70M barrels of oil per year are used to make polyester.[7]

Textile production uses about 93B cm³ of water per year, equivalent to 37M Olympic-sized swimming pools.[6]

The U.S. sends **3.8B POUNDS of APPAREL PER YEAR** to landfills.[3]

70 POUNDS PER AMERICAN[4]

CHANGE IN ANNUAL REVENUE[5]

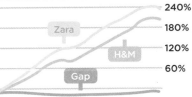

Zara — 240%
H&M — 180%
— 120%
Gap — 60%

2004 — 2015

MEAT
bad news on a bun

BEEF takes 28 times MORE LAND to produce than pork or chicken.[3]

MEAT CONSUMPTION OVER TIME[5]

CO₂ EMISSIONS PER KG OF FOOD[2]

Nuts .2 kg | Fish (wild catch) 3 kg | Chicken 6.1 kg | Beef 59.6 kg

About **6.7M** acres of tropical forests are bulldozed or burned for cattle production each year.[1]

Meat comsumption (million tons): 0–80

China
U.S.

1960 1970 1980 1990 2000 2010 2020

The world's top five meat and dairy producers combined emit more greenhouse gases than Exxon-Mobil, Shell, or BP.[4]

POPULATION GROWTH
BOOM making the planet go bust

Resources are **FINITE**, so people cannot be **INFINITE**.

WORLD POPULATION OVER TIME[2]

7.8B
6B
425M

People

In 2020, 267 BABIES were born every minute.[1]

1500 — 2000
Year

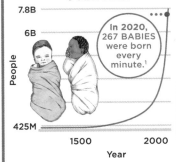

The Earth

Hey babe, need anything from the market?

Yes! Thanks! I'm running low on: land for growing crops, potable water, forests, fish

They...don't have that

CO₂ EMISSIONS
trapping heat, on repeat

In 1856, climate scientist Eunice Foote discovered the unique heat-trapping properties of CO₂.[1]

Global emissions must drop 7.6%/yr for next decade to meet 1.5°C warming target.[2]

You are here: **416 ppm**[4]

Pace of increase is increasing.

Other Energy 10%
Electricity and Heat Production 25%
Industry 21%
Transportation 14%
Buildings 6%
Agriculture and Land Use 24%

Global greenhouse gas emissions by energy-consuming sectors[3]

400 ppm
300 ppm
200 ppm
100 ppm

CO₂ in the atmosphere (parts per million, ppm)[5]

Emergence of homo sapiens

800,000 600,000 400,000 200,000 0
Years before present

I

Toxic, Meet Moxie

Mona Hanna-Attisha

Health Activist and Pediatrician at

Hurley Medical Center

The Erin Brockovich of Flint, Michigan

I AM ODDLY GOOD AT: puzzles

I AM ODDLY BAD AT: all domestic duties

MY GREATEST FEAR: not doing enough

THE TRAIT I MOST DEPLORE IN MYSELF: my gray hair

AN OCCASION WHEN I LIE: to protect my kids

A WORD OR PHRASE I MOST OVERUSE: "awesome"

A HABIT I'M TRYING TO GIVE UP: nail-biting

SOMETHING I USED TO DO BEFORE I REALIZED HOW BAD IT WAS FOR THE ENVIRONMENT: use lots of plastic

On April 25, 2014, city and state officials gathered at the Flint, Michigan, water treatment plant for a photo opportunity. The mayor counted down dramatically—five, four, three, two, one—and then pushed a black button, switching the city's water source from the Detroit Water and Sewage Department, which gets its water from Lake Huron and the Detroit River, to pulling from the Flint River. So much money would be saved by transitioning to the Karegnondi Water Authority, which was building a new pipeline and had a plan to transit the water more cheaply. This interim step using delicious and clean Flint River water was how the city would bridge the change during two years of construction, cheered government officials. For the cameras, Flint's mayor lifted his glass of Flint River water and took a gulp. He would come to wish he hadn't.

Pretty much immediately, Flint residents started reporting rust rims around their sinks and toilet bowls. Their tap water looked like pee, or worse. Demonstrations proliferated, with angry locals holding up bottles filled with yellow-brown water. Save a few "boil alerts" issued here and again, the mayor, city officials, and the governor ignored every cry.

Their tap water looked like pee, or worse.

At first, pediatrician Mona Hanna-Attisha was racing through rounds at Flint's public hospital, too busy to pay attention. If the government said the water was fine, the water must be fine, she told her childhood best friend, once an investigator at the Environmental Protection Agency, in August 2015 while catching up in Mona's backyard. Elin Warn Betanzo, the friend, shook her head. Elin had just moved back to Michigan from Washington, DC, where she'd been focused almost exclusively on water pollution issues. Once upon a time, Elin and Mona had been proud members of their high school's environmental club, mixing their "grungy, R.E.M.-listening, Doc Marten" vibe, as Mona put it, with real action like fighting to shut down an incinerator spewing toxic pollution one town over. They both retained their stay-and-fight attitudes. Elin had inside information showing that Flint's new water wasn't being properly treated. An essential anti-corrosion element wasn't being added, which meant Flint's water was likely leaching lead out of the water pipes, poisoning everyone in town.

Lead is a neurotoxin, meaning it affects the brain. In kids, it lowers IQ levels. In pregnant women, it can lead to miscarriage. There is no minimum safe threshold to stay below. The safe amount is zero. No amount of lead is ever remotely okay.

That night, Mona couldn't sleep. Every hour brought a new emotion: fear, disappointment, anxiety. By morning, the feelings had distilled into just one: anger.

The Flint children that Mona treated at the hospital had already been facing a long list of issues associated with poverty—crumbling schools, irregular diet, and unemployed parents. The idea that their most basic need, water, couldn't be met was unconscionable.

Then Mona had a breakthrough. She thought of a way to get to the bottom of the situation. When the Clean Water Act was passed in 1972, a requirement was instituted to protect the poorest, most vulnerable children. Because poisoning from lead paint was such a problem in old homes and buildings, all kids whose families were on Medicaid were to be blood-tested for lead at ages one and two. To Mona, this meant one thing: the ready existence of extensive lead-level blood tests for young Flint kids. She immediately contacted the Genesee County Health Department and requested the results of recent blood tests. But instead of having a helpful researcher call her back, she got a vague email suggesting that perhaps the county health department could start a study of lead levels in youth blood samples the following spring. The following spring? While kids continued to be poisoned for months and months? Her anger shot to fury.

She picked up the phone and called the state health department. A year earlier, she had met a nurse who worked in the department's

Childhood Lead Poisoning Prevention Program, and she had dug up her number. Unexpectedly, the woman answered. After hearing Mona out, she said that, well, yes, actually, they had observed a spike of late in the lead in blood tests. She would email Mona the data right away. All afternoon, Mona refreshed her email over and over, and all evening, and again all the next  day. But no data. Then, in a fit of rage, she had a flash of brilliance. Wait a minute, she could work this problem—prove a jump in lead levels—from inside her own hospital.

All county data was processed through the Hurley Medical Center, where she worked. She ordered a data dump of her clinic's pediatric patient data. She then set about figuring out which time periods exactly to compare, and how to deal data-wise with kids who had been tested multiple times. Just 270 kids had been tested in her clinic in the three months before the water changeover, and 71 since. Still, these numbers told a story, and it wasn't pretty. A tiny sample, yes, but lead in children under age five was up over 400 percent in the period following the switch to the Flint River, relative to the same period before.

Mona was tempted to pull the emergency brake right then, call the media and announce her findings. The consequences of delay were growing graver with every additional hour. But she knew that the larger her sample size, the more bulletproof her evidence. Yes, those 341 blood tests were ringing alarms, but getting a lead-level reading on every kid in Genesee County (where Flint River water now flowed from taps) would add much more heft. Her hospital came through. If she entered a formal research proposal requesting the results, and the review board sanctioned her study, she would get the numbers. At a big university, the process normally takes several months. But luckily, she worked at a small teaching hospital where decision-making could happen quickly. The reviewers at Hurley turned the request around in a day. Boom, she got her data. Now she had the results for two thousand tests. Depending on what age grouping she used, and which zip codes, she saw a jump in lead levels as large as 200 percent after the switchover.

"Do no harm" was part of Mona's Hippocratic oath as a doctor. But it wasn't just her medical background that had led her to this crucible moment. Mona had been born into a family of progressives and pacifists in Iraq. When her dad, an engineer, had been told he'd need to go to work making nuclear weapons for the repressive Ba'athist regime, he'd taken the family and fled, first to England, then to Michigan. Mona's parents didn't shield her from the harsh truth of chemical weapons attacks, air raids, and millions dead in the needless Iran-Iraq conflict. "We were always hoping to go back, thinking the time was coming, but then we never could," she reflected, sharing her backstory now, six years after she blew the whistle on Flint. She considers this family history her "superpower." "It gave me a heightened antenna for injustice," she said.

Several months into her lead-poisoning investigation, Mona learned that General Motors (GM) had quietly made a deal to switch away from Flint River water at their Flint plant. Reason: Flint River water had been corroding metal parts. Another rain cloud to add to Mona's gathering storm. Still, she worried the media and bureaucrats would find a way to make her look like the boy who cried wolf. She tried to imagine every possible way they might attack the facts that she had compiled. She ran her stats a dozen different ways, adjusting for factors like weather or instances of kids having multiple blood tests.

On September 24, 2015, just after one p.m., Mona stepped up to the mic in her hospital's conference room. For forty minutes, before a crowd of a hundred politicians, press, and distraught citizens, she slowly revealed the evidence. She explained, as Elin had told her back in August, that the Flint River water wasn't being treated to prevent lead pipe corrosion. She ended with a clear directive: an immediate switch to Lake Huron water was critical.

The blowback took mere minutes. The city's public relations (PR) head called the media, accusing Mona of "slicing and dicing" data. He deemed her conclusions "irresponsible." A counter-spin press conference was hastily arranged, and officials repeated in various forms: The water is safe. The water is in compliance. The water meets state and federal standards.

Only the work of an intrepid *Flint Journal* reporter digging into Mona's numbers and replicating her findings managed to turn the tide back toward truth. The reporter revealed so many cover-ups: city managers who had manipulated water tests to hide the lead; a regional water administrator who had said, by email, "I'm not so sure Flint is the community we want to go out on a limb for"; a Flint government office that was having bottled water delivered daily.

Flint families were back drinking Lake Huron water within weeks of Mona's announcement. But it would take until January 2021 for Rick Snyder, the governor of Michigan during the water crisis, to be charged with a federal crime—neglect of duty. The sentence, if he's convicted, could mean jail time.

The Flint water scandal is just one example of something far more pervasive—environmental racism.

Mona isn't stopping with Flint's enablers. To her, the Flint water scandal is just one example of something far more pervasive—environmental racism. In communities with low tax bases and poor, disenfranchised citizens, environmental protections are almost nil. There are still ten million lead pipes running through predominantly poor neighborhoods in the US. What happened in Flint would not have "happened in Birmingham or Grosse Pointe [rich, white communities]. Race and demographics played a part in this story," Mona stressed, as they do in so many other stories like it. She is pressing Congress and the US Food and Drug Administration (FDA) for policy upgrades and health-based lead standards. She's not merely a pediatric doctor anymore; she's a justice warrior.

FACT: In the 1890s near Sheffield, England, where Mona herself was born, lead in the water caused a rash of miscarriages. This initiated the use of a lead-based pill to prompt abortion.

FACT: Have you ever noticed that gas stations advertise and sell only unleaded gasoline? In the 1920s, Alice Hamilton, one of Mona's heroes, fought GM and Standard Oil to get lead out of gas because of the health hazard. Back then, she was called "hysterical," Mona explained. The change didn't happen until the 1970s.

Gregg Renfrew

Founder and Chief Executive Officer of

Beautycounter

Making "clean beauty" actually mean something

I AM ODDLY GOOD AT: dating advice

I AM ODDLY BAD AT: rolling my *R*s

MY GREATEST FEAR: flying

A GUILTY PLEASURE: Farmshop gluten-free chocolate chip cookies

THE TRAIT I MOST DEPLORE IN MYSELF: I talk way too fast.

AN OCCASION WHEN I LIE: when my husband asks me about new clothing I am wearing

MY GREATEST ACHIEVEMENT: my family

SOMETHING I USED TO DO BEFORE I REALIZED HOW BAD IT WAS FOR THE ENVIRONMENT: drink water out of plastic bottles all day

When Gregg Renfrew graduated from the University of Vermont in 1989, her mom gave her a monogrammed black leather briefcase and a $5,000 check. Her mom's message with the gift: "Good luck, and this is the last penny you'll get from me." Her mom wasn't being cold. She just needed to drill into her daughter that young women must learn to stand on their own two feet.

The money went fast, what with the deposit for her first New York City apartment and a shopping spree for work clothes, "which I did need," she said. But then she got a bit too comfy throwing down her credit card. Her $19,000 ad agency account exec salary barely covered basics; she quickly racked up $2,000 in debt. Despite warnings, she called her mom for a bailout. But Mom wasn't having it. "Well, I guess you'll need to get a higher-paying job," she said curtly.

Gregg had pretty much known this would be the response. It wasn't like she'd come from a feathered nest. By the time she'd left home for college, her parents had split up, her dad had struggled with cancer and lost his stock-trader job, and her mom had had to turn herself into a breadwinner. Gregg had emerged from these convulsions a fighter. But that didn't save her from the intoxicating pleasure of spending money she didn't have.

She knew her mom was right, so she went out and got herself a high-paying job at Xerox, selling copiers door-to-door in Manhattan's jewelry district. ("The same cutthroat territory where Starbucks CEO Howard Schultz began," Gregg crowed.) She was a natural. When her hard-nosed customers waffled over a price quote, Gregg would just walk away. The customers would then come running after her with their purchase orders, asking for a second chance. "They wanted to feel they had broken you," she said. Gregg was soon a nationwide top-seller.

The corporate ladder, though, was not her jam. She was scrappy. She liked identifying a problem and solving it. She liked making her own rules. This had been true since middle school. At twelve, she'd perfected the entrepreneurial side hustle, helping cater adult dinner parties. In college, she started a home-cleaning business on Nantucket, and scrubbed all summer long. "I needed a way to make money and still be at the beach when I could get a tan," she said. Postcollege, bridesmaid dresses for friends' weddings were bankrupting her, so that was her next business hack. She found better, cheaper options, then hocked those to her friends, then evolved that into a wedding registry business that she later sold to the multimedia home entertainment maven Martha Stewart. (Gregg, in typical form, actually talked back to the notoriously difficult tastemaker, and now her boss. "It drove Martha nuts," she said. In one example, Martha said, "Who picked that hideous blue pillow fabric?" and Gregg said, "You did, in our meeting yesterday afternoon.")

Her ballsy nature won her favors and a few lumps, too, as in 2006, when she took over as CEO of a faltering children's clothing brand owned by Suzy Hilfiger (then divorced from legendary retailer Tommy Hilfiger). Best & Co. needed financial discipline, and Gregg was hired to play the enforcer. Eighteen months later, she was fired. Publicly. She was speaking in front of sixty employees when the conference room door swung open. A messenger walked right up to her. "Are you Gregg Renfrew?" he inquired, and handed her an envelope. The note asked her to drop everything and "exit the building immediately." She cried for a week, did a lot of reflecting, and got over it. "I was too cocky," she said, rendering her verdict on the experience.

But something else was going to change everything. The same year she was hired at Best & Co., Gregg watched Al Gore's environmental documentary *An Inconvenient Truth* for the first time. She would never be the same.

The movie connected dots—friends struggling with infertility, her thirty-one-year-old nanny's cancer and death, damaged reefs. The movie terrified her. She purged all plastic from her home, swapped cleansers for vinegar, bought all organic. By this time, she was married with kids. The stakes were higher. The thought of potentially stunting her kids' development or causing cancer was too awful to contemplate. Then, one night in 2010, during the kids' nightly bubble bath, she wondered about the ingredients in the "natural foaming oatmeal wash" she was using. She dried her hands, grabbed her computer, found the website for the Environmental Working Group's Skin Deep database. Her "virtuous" purchase ranked eight out of ten for toxicity.

What other poisons was she rubbing all over her kids, and herself? She maniacally started checking lotions, sunscreen, toner and body-wash bottles and tubes. The smaller the print she read, the uglier things looked. She researched how cosmetics are regulated. They're not. Her research showed that not a single new regulation governing cosmetics had been passed in eighty-three years. When thousands of women reported sudden hair loss after using Wen hair products, the FDA did not pull the products from shelves. Unlike how a case of salmonella in bagged lettuce triggers an urgent recall, the FDA has no authority over cosmetics. Chemicals known to cause cancer or screw with hormones are at every CVS, Duane Reade, Walgreens, you name it.

Chemicals known to cause cancer or screw with hormones are at every CVS, Duane Reade, Walgreens, you name it.

Despite knowing "nothing about beauty, nothing about direct selling, nothing about nothing," Gregg got to work. She felt possessed. If safe products were nowhere to be found, she would make them. "The term 'clean beauty' didn't even exist yet," she said. Renfrew started making calls. She asked one friend at Estée Lauder, another at L'Oréal, all about their products. She found a chemist who then sent her to a "green chemist."

Three years later, she had formulations for a line of environmentally clean products and a manufacturer to make them.

By March 2013, Gregg and her tiny team had a collection of nine skin care products, and Beautycounter opened for business. The rush to launch frazzled her. Gregg planned a quick spring break getaway with her kids to regroup. In the hotel check-in line in the Bahamas, her phone started blowing up. The fresh rose water in their facial mist was turning moldy, according to employees holding down the fort. Instead of floral, the scent was eau de garbage. They had to call every purchaser, recall every bottle. "I was like, oh my God, we're dead in the water," Gregg said later. But this was the woman who'd talked back to Martha Stewart, who'd gotten fired ignominiously in front of her entire staff. She wasn't going to let a little recall upset the boat.

Today, Beautycounter is valued at $1 billion. Its products are pushed out by an army of environmental evangelists, almost all women, fifty thousand strong. The woman-to-woman direct sales model stems from that hard-won lesson from her mom: females need financial independence. Beautycounter empowers its "consultants"—aka salespeople—by having each of them run their own mini-business. The consultants' earnings are tied to exactly how much they personally sell, providing great incentive plus control. Getting started requires no cash outlay or special skills (the kind of gig Gregg's mom really could have used back in the day).

But success didn't make Gregg calmer about the environment, because she couldn't stop seeing the ugly, toxic, unpronounceable ingredients in major beauty brands next to hers. She started a list of ingredients she couldn't pronounce but kept seeing in products—butoxyethanol, sodium laureth sulfate, retinyl palmitate. She called it her "NeverList"—that is, these words would never appear on Beautycounter products. The list is now eighteen hundred chemicals long, and she shares it with anyone who asks.

But cockiness—again—was dangerous, even for Gregg, who was doing all the right things. That's because guaranteeing "clean" products is nearly impossible. Trace chemicals show up in ingredients where they are not supposed to (the case with one of Beautycounter's first products, which they scrapped and started again). Or a company supplying a clean ingredient ends up mistreating its employees. Basically, once you start unwinding the supply chain, asking where things are made, how they are mined, who works in the factories, how the ingredients are packaged, how they are shipped—things get really messy, really fast. The label "clean" on the package suddenly gets a lot trickier to stand behind.

Once you start unwinding the supply chain, asking where things are made, how they are mined, who works in the factories, how the ingredients are packaged, how they are shipped—things get really messy, really fast.

Take mica. Mica is the ingredient in eye shadow and lip gloss that creates that lovely shimmer effect. Much of mica is mined in India, Brazil, and China . . . often by kids. Kids digging in dark, airless pits, day and night. Gregg traveled to Jharkhand, India, to see for herself. She started backing a local organization fighting to end child labor in the area. She committed her Sustainability group, along with several independent auditors, to visit all the company's mica mining sites by the end of 2020, the first cosmetics company to do so, which Gregg's team accomplished. And over time, Beautycounter will move sourcing fully to Hartwell, Georgia, in the United States, where there are mines, and labor practices can be tracked more easily. At the same time, Gregg will continue to advocate for child welfare in the mining communities abroad. There is a similarly unsavory story attached to vanilla production. And on and on.

What Gregg wanted, in the end, was a revolution to confront all of it. And the monster lever that could bring so many toxic social and environmental practices to heel around the world? The US government.

This brought Gregg to a wood-paneled chamber in Washington, DC, in August 2019. In her scarlet high-necked silk blouse and horn-rimmed glasses, she stared down Committee Chairwoman Anna Eshoo, the congresswoman from California. Gregg was testifying before the Health Subcommittee of the House Committee on Energy and Commerce, demanding safer cosmetics laws. This was not her first attempt. She, her customers, and her consultants have held over 2,000 legislative meetings, placed 16,000 calls, sent 175,000 pleading emails. On the state level, in California, Gregg has had some political success. She's helped pass two bills, one requiring manufacturers to disclose fragrance ingredient information, as certain fragrances are toxic, and the other eliminating from personal-care products certain ingredients known to cause health harms. She wants politicians to be sick of seeing her. Sick enough to act.

> **FACT:** In Europe, roughly thirteen hundred toxic ingredients are banned from beauty products. In the US? Only eleven.

Detoxing Your Makeup Bag

On average, American women splash, rub, blend, blot, and lather on twelve beauty products daily, containing around 168 ingredients. Guess how many of those have been vetted at the federal level? Zippo. Avoiding hazards requires becoming a private investigator. Here's help:

Remain skeptical. Many claims like "clean" and "organic" are meaningless because there are no standards. Companies have been known to remove chemicals with a bad rap, like bisphenol A (BPA), but replace them with something as bad or even worse.

Make the Environmental Working Group (EWG.org) your new best friend. This watchdog's Skin Deep database ranks seventy-seven thousand personal-care products on a scale from 1 to 10 based on chemicals of concern. Currently, just 2 percent of the products reviewed have received their EWG Verified stamp of approval. See where your stash ranks, and toss accordingly.

Be discerning with hair straighteners, fragrances/perfumes, dark permanent hair dye, skin lighteners, loose powders. These notoriously contain toxins.

Download the Detox Me app, from the Silent Spring Institute. Use in stores to scan product barcodes before buying. If a safer option is available, the app will let you know.

Avoid products with "fragrance" or "parfum" on the label. When "fragrance" is listed as an ingredient, it's usually a blend of various ingredients and chemical compounds. Often suppliers seek to protect fragrances as trade secrets, and there is no way to know for sure what ingredients are in the formulas—this is also known as the "fragrance loophole." Chemicals that may commonly be found in fragrances, like phthalates, have been linked to endocrine disruption, which means they have the potential to interfere with the body's hormones.

Go for "phthalate free" and "paraben free."

Pop into one of Credo Beauty's stores to toss old eye shadow, blush, face lotion, and more in exchange for Credo reward points. Because of the varying sizes and material makeup (i.e., the metal springs and plastic in a pump dispenser) of most cosmetics packaging, these containers usually fall outside the scope of traditional recycling. Credo has a way to recycle them, sending all they collect off to TerraCycle, a business managing to recycle the typically non-recyclable. Credo, which has assembled the Dirty List, with twenty-seven hundred no-use ingredients, will also book a consultation with you online, over Zoom, or in the store to help audit your makeup bag (though this service costs money).

Begin swapping out your everyday products like deodorant, face moisturizer, and sunscreen. As your current products run out, switch to clean ones.

Text BETTERBEAUTY to 52886 (in the US) to urge Congress to pass clean-beauty laws. This is Beautycounter's effort—join them!

Michelle Zhu
Cofounder and Chief Executive Officer

Tammy Hsu
Cofounder and Chief Scientific Officer

Huue

Making "green" blue jeans with biotechnology

I AM ODDLY GOOD AT: identifying voices of female pop stars (Michelle) // taking fast showers (Tammy)

I AM ODDLY BAD AT: Bike riding—I once fell off a stationary bike. // walking quietly

MY GREATEST FEAR: leaving potential unrealized // losing my memory

A GUILTY PLEASURE: old chick flicks like *What a Girl Wants* and *27 Dresses* (They're so cheesy.) // browsing travel sites for imaginary vacations

THE TRAIT I MOST DEPLORE IN MYSELF: being a people pleaser // I wish I were better at small talk and connecting to new people.

AN OCCASION WHEN I LIE: I used to feel pressure to pretend I knew things to seem smart, but now I've realized it's easier to just be honest about feelings of uncertainty. // when the truth won't help anyone, and will only hurt

A HABIT I'M TRYING TO GIVE UP: going to bed past midnight // sugary snacks

SOMETHING I USED TO DO BEFORE I REALIZED HOW BAD IT WAS FOR THE ENVIRONMENT: buy a lot of fast fashion // throw away food scraps rather than composting

When the first pair of blue jeans was made in 1873 by Levi Strauss, the denim-blue hue came from crushed indigo plant leaves. Indigo had been a prized crop since antiquity, the dye being difficult to get and once reserved for royalty. Then, in 1865, a German scientist figured out how to mix up the color chemically, and plant-based indigo became history.

Today that reality is painfully obvious in southern China, near Xintang, where there are rivers that run a midnight black. The dye runoff from billions of blue jeans swirls in the water, so potent that it can change the sex of a fish. These waterways are so toxic, a thrown match could light them on fire. One out of every three pairs of the planet's jeans are made in the region. Skinny, boyfriend, low-rise, distressed, you name it. All made with a chemical mixture of—among other nasty ingredients—aniline (poisonous petroleum byproduct), cyanide (poison), and formaldehyde (poison). Making one part indigo requires one hundred parts petroleum. Then, to make it dissolve in water, you need to mix in a chemical harsh enough to corrode metal.

The dye runoff from billions of blue jeans swirls in the water, so potent that it can change the sex of a fish.

Yes, your fave double-cuffed, ripped-in-just-the-right-place jeans are a major environmental hazard. Really, clothing dye of any kind is a problem. Twenty percent of the world's water pollution is caused by clothing and fabric dyeing, according to a 2019 World Bank report.

This is precisely what had Michelle Zhu prepping so madly in April 2019. She was in Los Angeles, about to walk into the most important meeting of her life. She double-checked her one and only sample. She reviewed her slides and questions. With only forty-five precious minutes, she needed a tight script. She wished her business partner, bioengineer Tammy Hsu, could be there with her, because Tammy was the scientist who'd invented the technical parts of their business idea.

With Tammy's blessing and notes, Michelle would have to face Adriano Goldschmied—the "godfather of premium denim"—on her own. Heard of AG jeans? That's Adriano Goldschmied. A fashion legend who shaped denim lines at Diesel, Replay, and Gap.

Michelle and Tammy's preparations paid off. The forty-five-minute meeting stretched to three hours, and really, AG would have stayed all night. Michelle was blowing his mind. Her pitch? She and Tammy would eliminate the toxic waste from denim by making colors with safe dyes. How? Bioengineering.

Tammy had discovered the new dye-making technique unexpectedly five years earlier. She'd been working with her PhD lab group at UC Berkeley, studying processes inside cells. Many scientists who work with cells use color that becomes activated only when certain chemical changes occur inside the cell. This way a researcher knows a reaction has happened even if it can't be seen with the eye. To make this color, the lab group mixed a strand of DNA that coded for the color-rich indigo plant with a bit of bacteria. The bacteria they used is best known for its association with food poisoning—E. coli. What's potentially dangerous about E. coli is that it divides really quickly, creating more of itself. But when it comes to pumping out more and more dye with each division, that speedy bacterial growth is really, really handy.

Tammy's team hadn't realized how powerful this technique could be for making dye. And their success with it quickly eclipsed their main project. Where might this invention lead? No one quite knew.

Inspired by her professor, Tammy applied to an incubator called IndieBio, which is dedicated to helping launch biology-based ventures. Incubators are basically professional support groups that are choosy about who they let participate and that provide mentorship, networking opportunites, and funding. The IndieBio team loved Tammy. They thought her dye technique was truly revolutionary and would be embraced by manufacturers around the world. But to get accepted into the program, Tammy would need a partner; IndieBio insisted that two founders were fundamental to business success.

Lucky coincidence. Tammy's lab mate was engaged to a savvy business brain named Michelle Zhu who had literally just told him she was itching to start a company from scratch. She was working in strategy and operations at Yelp but was ready to leave if an opportunity arose.

The match couldn't have been more tailor-made. While Tammy is soft-spoken, creative (as a kid, she designed everything from robots to American Girl doll clothes), and deep in the weeds of science, Michelle is an extrovert overachiever who can spin a winning sales pitch on cue. Michelle was even raised around jeans manufacturing. Her Chinese parents ran a fashion brand in Los Angeles after moving there from China when Michelle was three. On work trips with her dad back to China, where the clothes were made, she had seen those polluting factories up close.

Michelle and Tammy started spending every waking moment in their basement lab space at IndieBio. "We didn't live together but we might as well have," Michelle said. They named their company Tinctorium, after the *Indigofera tinctoria* plant that produces indigo.

Listening to Michelle's presentation, AG, the denim maestro, understood immediately that this was "the solution to change" his industry.

Now Michelle and Tammy run their own lab, where they brew up small batches of dye from bioengineered bacteria. Each vat resembles an oversized blender—with tubes going every which way. If the dye is produced efficiently and is adequately absorbed into little squares of test cloth, and the color is right, they keep working with that recipe, tweaking factors like temperature and nutrients to improve output. Key to the whole operation is the fact that the dye can be used in existing machinery at dye mills and factories, so Michelle and Tammy are spared building their own dye facilities. In 2019, they changed their name to Huue, which they felt better represented their mission of creating a rainbow of sustainable colors.

As if AG's support wasn't enough, in 2020, Huue got a great jolt of confidence, winning $1 million in a female founders competition sponsored by Melinda Gates's fund that invested alongside several other funds. Even more exciting was an investment from the Nobel Prize–winning scientist Jennifer Doudna, who invented CRISPR (the buzzy gene-editing technique currently making headlines).

There are still hurdles ahead. Huue needs to scale up from ten-liter vats of dye to the industrial-sized vats that the big players use. They know what to do—but making this happen technically is going to require plenty of tinkering. Their investors believe it's possible and have total confidence in Tammy and Michelle. Meanwhile, AG has offered them a business model they can duplicate around the world: they handle the dye process, the jeans companies provide the pants, and together they create a label to tout the revolutionary planet-saving approach used to make the earth-friendly jeans. Plenty of companies are already knocking. "We have the attention of a lot of the world's leading denim brands," Michelle said assuredly.

Huue is aiming to see its first thousand pairs of blue jeans roll into stores sometime in 2021. Then, in the future, there will be lots more jeans, but they might not be blue. The next frontier for Huue will be using this process to make all colors—orange, purple, green. . . . "Culture nature's rainbow. That's our mission," says Michelle.

> **FACT:** Ironically, the reason that indigo is so desirable for jeans is because it is such a lame dye. Rather than penetrate the fabric like most coloring, the indigo sticks to the outside of the thread. With use and washing, bits flake off, revealing some white thread beneath. This creates that cool worn-in look that only jeans have.

> **FACT:** Your wide-leg jeans release 56,000 fibers (on average) when washed, according to a 2020 University of Toronto study. That's roughly ten times the number of fibers released when a fleece jacket gets laundered. The research team was investigating why so many fabric fibers were polluting the oceans and waterways.

> **FACT:** The number of fashion seasons has increased from two a year—spring/summer and fall/winter—to as many as 50 to 100 micro-seasons, according to the 2015 film *True Cost.*

FACT: In Xintang, the town in Guangdong Province, China, that claims to be the "jeans capital of the world," 200,000 garment workers in 3,000 factories and workshops produce almost 300 million pairs of jeans annually—800,000 pairs a day, according to *Fashionopolis* by journalist Dana Thomas.

Growing Color

Women around the world are harnessing bacteria to reimagine how products are colored. Laura Luchtman and Ilfa Siebenhaar run a Netherlands-based lab called Living Colour that focuses on strains of bacteria that naturally produce pigment. The women grow bacteria harvested from soil, water, and even skin, and have been trying to expose bacteria to sound frequencies in order to prompt the bacteria to create patterns on fabric.

Natsai Audrey Chieza at her Faber Futures design studio in London noticed that the bacteria *Streptomyces coelicolor* makes a striking red-purple pigment. She started growing the bacteria directly on silk, creating bold, colorfast colors.

Catherine Coleman Flowers

Environmental Health Activist and Founder of
the Center for Rural Enterprise and
Environmental Justice

Exposing an American horror story
of human waste and neglect

I AM ODDLY GOOD AT: genealogy

I AM ODDLY BAD AT: threading a needle

I ADMIRE: water walkers

THE TRAIT I MOST DEPLORE IN MYSELF: I do not deplore anything about myself.

AN OCCASION WHEN I LIE: about my weight

A WORD OR PHRASE I MOST OVERUSE: "You know . . ."

A HABIT I'M TRYING TO GIVE UP: eating crackers

I WISH I HAD LEARNED WHEN I WAS YOUNG: to fly

Catherine Flowers has taken on the stuff that stinks. So get ready for a messy story here.

Sometime today, nature will call, and if you happen to be at school, you will probably scroll on your phone as you spend a few minutes in a graffiti-scribbled stall. Afterward, you will flush, the toilet will grumble and swirl, and all will happily disappear.

The waste will then flow through buried pipes to the local wastewater treatment plant. There, the solids and liquids separate, added chemicals kill the viruses and bacteria, the liquids seep into the ground, and the "sludge" that won't break down goes to a landfill or facility to become fuel or fertilizer. No fuss, no muss.

Well, some people do not get to just flush and forget.

Some people do not get to just flush and forget.

Catherine Flowers works for those people. Calling her a saint would make sense.

Get this. Here in the richest nation on earth, where we sequence DNA and blast rockets to Mars, we can't manage to guarantee this simple dignity. Catherine, for twenty years, has been agitating for Alabamans who are literally living in their own human waste. Living in places with no nearby treatment plant, in some cases because the land was once enslaved people's territory and so was never officially incorporated. Sometimes the home is just too remote. A backyard septic tank can solve the problem, except that these tanks are totally unaffordable for some people. So the flies come. Along with disease. And terrible shame.

In Lowndes County, Alabama, where Catherine grew up, toilet waste pours out of straight pipes into peoples' yards, forming aboveground cesspools out back. Clumps of sopped toilet paper cling where yard toys should be. Sometimes the sewage backs up in the pipes inside, reappearing later in sinks and tubs—anything but flushed and forgotten.

A quiet force who these days says she is too busy even for house plants, Catherine grew up in a concrete-block house smack on the route of the famous 1965 Selma-to-Montgomery voting rights march. Lowndes was a county "where not a single Black person was registered to vote despite being majority of the population," she emphasized. Catherine's location and this history have everything to do with where life has led her.

Catherine's family was poor. During much of her upbringing, she used "slop jars" or an outhouse as her bathroom. Her mom drove the school bus and was a teacher's aide, and her dad stocked shelves on a military base until a back injury sidelined him. She and her brothers had a "pool table" they crafted from two stacked soda crates. They used marbles for balls.

Her parents were organizers, and evening gatherings around her dining table with notable civil rights activists like Stokely Carmichael were common. Catherine's mom had another reason to get political. She was the victim of an unthinkable abuse, being sterilized (an operation so women can no longer get pregnant) without her consent while still in the hospital after having Catherine's brother. This happened in the very same hospital where hundreds of unknowing Black men believed they were receiving medical care when in fact they were guinea pigs in a study of untreated syphilis, in the now infamous, ethically abusive Tuskegee medical experiments.

In elementary school, Catherine was already showing sensitivity to wrongs. She cried when the voice on the loudspeaker announced that Martin Luther King Jr. had been shot. As a teen, she spoke out when she recognized that her school did not resemble the white schools nearby. Desks were broken, students did not read at grade level, and their counselor never bothered to mention the SAT test. She was particularly bugged by her school's name: Lowndes County Training School. She noticed how "Training School" was tacked on to Black schools' names to signal that these were subpar places. "I didn't want my diploma to say that," recalls Catherine.

She wrote poetry, which got her noticed and tapped to become a youth fellow at the Robert F. Kennedy Memorial Foundation. She spent a summer with the prestigious program in Washington, DC, studying issues of school segregation. When she returned home, she challenged her school's name—and won. She demanded an investigation of various educational practices, like unequal allocated school resources based on race. Under pressure, the district superintendent resigned. As the traditional class gift that seniors leave to the school, Catherine organized a sign with her school's new name.

She wanted to attend Howard University and was accepted, but her parents couldn't afford the steep tuition. Instead, she enrolled in nearby Talladega College, and later transferred to Alabama State University. Ultimately, she became a history teacher, teaching current events and civil rights law to high school students in Washington, DC, North Carolina, and Detroit. Catherine was renowned for taking her students on fantastic field trips, once to the great Apollo Theater in Harlem. Other classes she brought to Alabama, one time to participate in the thirty-fifth anniversary of the Selma-to-Montgomery march.

After that visit, one of her former teachers, hearing that Catherine had come, called her with a desperate plea: "Things are worse for us than they have ever been. Please come back and help."

How could Catherine refuse that? These were her people. In 2000, Catherine moved back to Alabama. She quickly saw that the inequity that had spurred the 1960s uprising continued. Human waste festered behind houses and trailer homes. Homeowners were sometimes evicted—or worse, arrested—for the crime of not treating their toilet waste. Catherine recognized that this was environmental injustice, every bit as bad as providing unequal schools or denying Black people the vote.

This was environmental injustice, every bit as bad as providing unequal schools or denying Black people the vote.

The problem ran layers deep. In poor rural counties, there is frequently no government-provided wastewater treatment. Home septic systems cost $10,000 to $25,000, more than most Lowndes residents earn in a full year. Some residents begged and borrowed and purchased a home septic tank, only to have it fail. The mud-like consistency of the soil that makes the region ideal for growing cotton makes septic systems go haywire. Normally, the solids sink and the liquids drain into the ground. Here, the thick clay holds the liquid, so the systems frequently back up.

Catherine saw that the area was a cesspool of injustice every bit as nasty as those that riddled backyards, with poverty at the center. The only way out was through economic development—better jobs and higher pay. She wooed an economic development expert, Robert Woodson Sr., from Washington, DC, to help get to work on that. She got his attention by traveling to a conference she learned he would be attending and then cornering him with her story. Woodson traveled to Lowndes, and Catherine gave him an unforgettable tour.

He was barely back inside his hotel room post-tour when he called his reporter pal at the *Washington Post* to share what he had witnessed. The friend published a column about Lowndes's rampant raw waste. Catherine Flowers's cause was instantly a national story.

In 2009, on a visit in the backyard of a pregnant woman facing arrest for inadequate waste disposal, Flowers was attacked by mosquitoes. She broke out in a full-body rash. Two different doctors declared her fine. "I asked one, 'Is it possible that I have something that American doctors are not trained to look for?' Because they don't even acknowledge that there's a raw sewage problem," she said. Catherine couldn't help wondering what diseases were festering where she was regularly standing.

So, when she came across a *New York Times* editorial by an infectious disease expert on "the forgotten diseases of forgotten people," she gasped. The Baylor College of Medicine professor exposed that tropical diseases believed confined to the "Third World" were the "new plague of poverty" in America. He described larval pork tapeworms leading to seizures and epilepsy, murine typhus linked to rodent infestations, a "kissing bug" resembling a cockroach that feeds on human blood.

Catherine didn't even reach the end of the editorial before contacting the Baylor scientist. "What inspired you to write?" she asked. His reply: "I was hoping a Catherine Flowers would reach out to me." Yes, he was hoping to interest an invested activist exactly like her.

He immediately sent a parasitologist to crisscross Lowndes County with Catherine, gathering blood and stool samples. With fifty-five full sample vials in hand, Catherine rented a car and delivered them personally to the lab in Houston—these were precious specimens. The results came quickly. A shocking 34 percent showed *Necator americanus*, a parasite that is a species of hookworm that lives in the intestine, feeding on blood.

What happened next really set Catherine on fire. Rather than jump to help, the Alabama Department of Public Health issued a statement announcing zero evidence of hookworm. "I wasn't all that surprised," Catherine quipped about the cover-up. "I had come to expect this." Catherine enlisted a legal aid nonprofit, Earthjustice, to file a federal civil rights complaint. (As of April 2021, she was still waiting for an investigation.)

Catherine intensified her campaign. She hit up all nine Alabama congresspeople for federal assistance funds. When her request to meet was turned down, she would just show up anyway. She had learned that the politicians have to leave their offices eventually, so if you are sitting in the waiting areas, you can snag them. She got to know Bryan Stevenson; she even skipped her annual mammogram appointment to accept an invitation to meet him. Lucky she did, because the revered activist lawyer behind the Equal Justice Initiative gave her a job offer on the spot.

Over time, her star started rising, and she got more and more visibility. In 2015, when the fiftieth anniversary of the Selma-to-Montgomery march came, she was given the prime pulpit of the historic AME Church where that famed 1965 march began. She preached that environmental injustice and poverty intersected in the sewage that flowed from forgotten people's homes. She preached that 1.7 million Americans still lack basic plumbing. She hosted a *National Geographic* film crew, who were treated to the bulging eyes of frogs peeking through a pit of human sewage.

She was asked to interview climate guru Al Gore on the big stage celebrating the 2018 opening of the National Memorial for Peace and Justice in Montgomery, Alabama. "It was my 'Oprah moment,'" she said. Soon Bernie Sanders called. In May 2019, she testified before Congress about hookworm, which she had now found in Missouri, California, and several rural pockets across the United States. Iconic actress and rabble-rouser (she's still getting arrested protesting climate inaction) Jane Fonda joined the board of her organization, the Center for Rural Enterprise and Environmental Justice.

When Sanders's presidential bid ended and Joe Biden became the

Democratic candidate, Biden added her to his environmental task force. In October 2020, the MacArthur Foundation called and awarded her the mega prestigious "genius grant"—major street cred plus $625,000. The first thing she did after that call? "I danced right there in my bedroom," she said. Now she's published her own book, *Waste: One Woman's Fight Against America's Dirty Secret,* and has been profiled in the *New Yorker.*

Catherine is on her own march for justice. She doesn't plan on stopping anytime soon.

> **FACT:** On average, humans produce three hundred twenty pounds of waste per person each year according to Kim Barrett, a professor of medicine at University of California, San Diego.

II

What a Waste

Anna Brightman

Cofounder of

UpCircle

Turning food byproducts into cool products

I AM ODDLY GOOD AT: sewing

I AM ODDLY BAD AT: all racket sports! (I blame it on not being sure if I am right- or left-handed . . .)

MY GREATEST FEAR: When you get down to the end of a carrot or something you're grating, I freak out that I might accidentally grate my finger!!

THE TRAIT I MOST DEPLORE IN MYSELF: I'm really bad at letting things go.

A GUILTY PLEASURE: Listening to overly angry music while running. I'm also obsessed with crime, criminals, and criminal justice systems!! If you browsed my Netflix "suggestions for you," you'd probably think I was a tad strange.

A TIME I'D RATHER NOT REMEMBER: Probably around the age of thirteen or fourteen, I was a real nightmare.

IF I COULD CHANGE ONE HUMAN BEHAVIOR TO SAVE THE PLANET: The "meat and two veg" approach to how we plan meals. The centerpiece to every meal doesn't need to be meat or fish.

Sometimes, older brothers can actually be useful.

Anna Brightman's brother, William, entered a bustling coffee shop near Covent Garden in central London in 2016, for his morning jolt of strong coffee. The line for this indie brew was long, winding through the shop and out the door. So many coffee addicts. William watched the baristas flying behind the counter, sweating to keep up with demand, blasting steam into milk, banging spent coffee grounds into trash buckets—thwack, thwack, thwack! A mound of steaming brown sludge for every cup served. So much coffee. So much sludge. "Where does all that waste go?" he wondered aloud. The tattooed guy behind the counter shrugged. Nowhere good, he replied. Nowhere good.

William brought this info back to his sister, twenty-two-year-old Anna, a budding makeup artist.

William shared the research he'd done after speaking to the barista. The coffee shop produced so much sludge—aka soaked coffee grounds— and they had to pay the city for every sack they put out for pickup. That collection went to the landfill, where the grounds rotted (much like all those wasted avocados on page 268), emitting methane, that gas that is, yep, twenty times more damaging than carbon dioxide in contributing to

global warming. Multiply this by all of England's wasted coffee grounds, and you have about five hundred thousand tons of arabica making trouble each year (for a visual, that's a pile of around forty thousand double-decker buses).

As Anna listened to her brother, she thought of the cosmetics gurus she'd watched obsessively on YouTube throughout her teens, who'd explained how coffee is loaded with antioxidants and has super anti-inflammatory properties. They'd even said that used grounds could make blood vessels close up, making them great at removing redness from skin, which was why the grounds were becoming very trendy to use in Australia. "You've probably heard of free radicals. They're kind of like tiny bouncy balls in your body, flying around indiscriminately and smashing up the furniture. Caffeine removes these from your system, meaning your skin cells stay in top condition for longer," she explained. A whiz at face glitter who regularly wore five shades of eye shadow at once, Anna began to wonder if those five hundred thousand tons of wasted coffee might make a girl (or boy) look "smart" if applied in just the right way.

William loved his sister's way of thinking. They hit the kitchen, busting out blenders and bowls. They tested formulations, trying all kinds of ratios and ingredients with the grounds. Their first prototype was an exfoliant scrub that made use of the coffee's coarse texture. In powdery form, it was a disaster—not because it didn't work but because, well, picture a bathroom covered in soot or garden soil. The powder was too loose and went everywhere. So, they whipped in shea butter. Solved. William and Anna liked the results on their own skin, so they called up friends and got them to try it.

Friends asked for more, please.

A year went by. The Brightman sibs were convinced they had an eco-business worth pursuing. Not only were they diverting waste, but, if their idea really took off, the coffee grounds might also be the perfect replacement for plastic microbeads, another environmental scourge. The tiny plastic bits—found in traditional face scrubs (and so many other products you use)—were known to circle down drains, enter rivers and oceans, then fish stomachs, and ultimately humans, doing god-knows-what to our systems. Britain eventually banned microbeads in 2016, joining the US, which had done so in 2015.

But a few prototypes of a homemade coffee scrub weren't enough to turn the heads of big business. They needed to expand. So began the era of Anna and William and the Weekend Baristas. Every Saturday and Sunday for the next two years, the siblings could be found navigating their dad's beat-up dark blue Citroën—squeaky brakes, no ventilation or heat, windows stuck down—across London. They went from café to café, begging baristas to please save their grounds—and carefully. "If they go tossing in a mint leaf, or a banana peel, then the whole batch is ruined," Anna said. She was usually frozen stiff by the end of a trip. She found herself wishing she drank coffee, especially when she saw William dash inside a café with the white collection buckets and exit with a steaming cup of joe for himself. But she'd never liked the stuff. It was an acquired taste that to her just tasted bitter. "I hated it the way many kids hate olives, horseradish, mustard."

Five years later, in 2021, they are still making these regular pickups. The beater car eventually died and was replaced by a company-owned van. And they have help now, too. Some eight employees who, in addition to managing manufacturing that they outsource to a local plant, drive to some one hundred London coffee shops, every single day, for pickups. Grounds turn rancid quickly, so the team is always in a race against the clock. They gather the slurry one day and must "upcycle"—manufacture it into facial scrub—by the very next day.

None of this happened in a straight line, however. It took Anna several years to figure out what she was supposed to be when she grew up and how the coffee grounds and facial scrubs fit into the grand plan. The teachers at her fancy all-girls high school ("very results driven and high-pressured") insisted that she pursue "a real profession" at university. Anna tried—she chose art history as her major at the University of York, then worked in fashion PR right after—but, chatty and colorful in her side ponytails and swingy Indian earrings, she just didn't fit any traditional path.

> *The teachers at her fancy all-girls high school insisted that she pursue "a real profession" at university.*

Trying to position herself for a more practical business path, she applied for a management position at a massive grocery chain. She was twenty-one years old. Most of the employees had kids her age. At her final interview for the job, the big boss took her aside, tossed her application down on the table, and then ripped into her: "You've done art history at university, and you are twenty-one with basically no experience. How dare you apply when you are clearly utterly unqualified?" Rather than wilt, Anna whipped back that he was "dead wrong," arguing that there was more to the job than academic smarts and mathematical equations. "This is a people job and needs someone likable with people smarts."

He excused her to a waiting taxi. "I totally blew it," she vented to her mom, calling her from the car. But she was wrong. The big boss called with a job offer that same day. Their final exchange had been a setup. Her confident pushback to his aggressive no had been just what he'd needed to hear from someone who would oversee his 116 stores. "I love being the boss," she says, beaming, remembering her fifteen months running the chain, entrusted with all that responsibility.

Her brother, William, meanwhile, had graduated from Oxford University with an economics degree and thrown himself into high finance. He was a born risk-taker and natural entrepreneur; his mind, though, kept wandering back to the coffee wastage.

They found time to nurture the idea, despite their day jobs. As their excitement for their concept grew, their product development intensified. They mixed in scented oils, testing combinations like lemongrass and mint, lemon and black pepper, clove and cinnamon. They sought out only natural ingredients with pronounceable names that were vegan, nontoxic, and earth-friendly. But a nagging question still tugged: How many people—besides their nearest and dearest—would rub their faces with a thick mousse made from coffee grounds?

They needed to find out.

They booked a booth at the London Coffee Festival in the event's "Innovation Hall." Cranking up production—which was still happening in the kitchen of their childhood home and increasingly expanding across the whole top floor of the house—they stockpiled hundreds of scrubs, plenty for the five-day show. The good news: no one was the least bit ruffled about exfoliating with coffee refuse. The bad news: their little silver tins were sold out on day one.

At a cosmetics showcase months later, their booth was buzzing with buyers. Anna tried to meet everyone who walked by, but there were so many. "I'm quite keen on your scrubs," a woman announced, shoving a card at Anna; she had to dash out but hoped Anna would call her. Anna tossed the card into her tote. It was days later when she dug it out. Turns out the woman was a buyer for Urban Outfitters, their dream retailer. "Of course, we started harassing her," Anna admits. When they connected, the buyer did not mince words: I suggest you rethink branding and packaging, she said. Still, the woman placed a small order for six of her stores. Huzzah!

The feedback from the Urban Outfitters buyer made an impression. Yes, their branding was off. Their name back then, Optiat, while clever—the letters stood for "Other People's Trash Is Another's Treasure"—conjured up eye products. They renamed themselves UpCircle. "UpCircle" because the goal was to create circular products, meaning doing away with the idea of waste, because once one use is done, there is a next use. They were in the business, too, of upcycling, a better end for trash, rather than the typical "take, make, waste," a common Anna refrain.

They were in the business, too, of upcycling, a better end for trash, rather than the typical "take, make, waste."

The date to unveil their new look to Urban Outfitters was looming. A passel of bendable aluminum tubes arrived, allowing Anna and William to fill the order. But, upon closer examination, they saw that none of the new tubes were labeled or could be sealed at the bottom after filling. How would they seal and label their tubes without industrial equipment? After a period of panic, William and Anna did what they'd always done—improvise. Manual tube-folding and labels made on a home printer would have to do. "They looked like a fourteen-year-old's art project," said Anna. Luckily, Urban Outfitters didn't blink.

Their momentum continued to build. In 2018, the Brightmans were invited onto the BBC's *Dragons' Den,* Britain's version of *Shark Tank.* Despite giving a load of criticism—about leaky tubes, crooked labels—three judges were itching to invest. They loved the Brightmans' originality. They loved that coffee grounds would clean complexions and not dirty the planet. In a scrub, the grounds washed down the drain and decomposed, while in a landfill without oxygen, they rotted and produced methane. But Anna and William turned the offer down. They felt it was too low—that's how bullish they were about what they were up to. Instead, UpCircle scored a loan from England's savviest entrepreneur, Virgin Group's Sir Richard Branson, the magnate behind Virgin Air, Virgin Records, and Virgin Megastore. Following that, the Brightmans raised $280,000 in a crowdfunding campaign.

Coffee grounds were just the start for UpCircle. A chai tea manufacturer offered Anna his used leaves. Those became soaps, in striking scents like cardamom and star anise. Apricot and other stone fruit pits, ground up, contain powerful minerals. They form the base of a new mineral-rich formula for UpCircle balms and creams. New ideas surface every day. Fruit juicers happily offload mandarin and kiwi waters that evaporate (but can be captured) when the juicers make concentrate. Those are beneficial in toner or a spritz. The Brightmans are starting to work with lemon rinds, to be made into hand sanitizer, and are exploring collecting scattered flower petals swept up from wedding venues and florists. Coffee oils in the grounds—once extracted—are keystones of hydrating face serums.

To date, the Brightmans have proudly spared landfills one thousand tons of coffee grounds. Their products are on the shelves of mainstream British retailers like Topshop, Boots, and Sainsbury's. In March 2020, Ulta Beauty brought UpCircle to the US for the first time. Credo, known for its tough eco standards, now sells a line of UpCircle products. Anna and William are clearly succeeding, but Anna says she won't feel like the planet is winning until UpCircle can "push less sustainable brands off the shelf."

As for working day and night alongside her brother, it's "brilliant and awful at the same time," she quips with a knowing smirk.

FACT: Bio-bean, a London-based company, is turning coffee grounds into fuel—barbecue coals, fire logs, and biomass pellets. The idea started when a student noticed the film of oil collecting on top of a cold Americano coffee and wondered, with that slick, could this be burned as fuel? The first product was a compact fire log made from the grounds of twenty-five cups of coffee. The company is even exploring the possibility of selling these pellets back to coffee shops to be used to roast coffee or boil water, which would create a truly circular economy, with waste becoming the input power for the production activities that created it.

Kaitlin Mogentale

Founder and Chief Executive Officer of

Pulp Pantry

A leftovers lifesaver

I AM ODDLY GOOD AT: speaking

I AM ODDLY BAD AT: baking (I get too experimental.)

MY GREATEST FEAR: mediocrity

A GUILTY PLEASURE: sleeping copious amounts

THE TRAIT I MOST DEPLORE IN MYSELF: bossiness

AN OCCASION WHEN I LIE: to hype others up

MY GREATEST ACHIEVEMENT: cultivating resilience and tenacity

A TIME I'D RATHER NOT REMEMBER: the days spent concerned about what others think

SOMETHING I USED TO DO BEFORE I REALIZED HOW BAD IT WAS FOR THE ENVIRONMENT: eat like the midwesterner that I am

Whrrrrr . . . down the neck of the pulverizer they went, one after another, the base of the next carrot used to push the prior one farther inside. Kaitlin

Mogentale was engrossed in watching a bagful of carrots disappear into a few shot glasses' worth of juice. So many carrots in, so little juice out. She was with her college friend who was way into juicing. (What else would you expect at the University of Southern California?)

When the motor stopped, the collection bin on one side of the machine was stuffed full of stringy orange gunk. Kaitlin peered inside, catching a whiff that smelled earthy and sweet. "Mmmmmm," she cooed. Her friend quickly detached the waste container and banged the contents out into the trash. Wait! Kaitlin wanted to scream. That's all the good stuff . . . half the nutrients . . .

Kaitlin was primed to both ooh and aah and get testy over a pile of vitamin-rich carrot remains. For the few months before, Kaitlin had biked over to a community garden twice a week to teach a class of wiggly kids about growing and cooking fresh produce. The job was the internship portion of her social entrepreneurship class. They squealed as they shoved their fingers into the wormy soil or tasted a just-picked tomato, the seeds bursting into their cheeks. Farm-fresh veggies were as foreign to most of them as igloos. Many had never seen a homegrown tomato. These kids usually pulled some Sour Patch Kids or potato chips out of their backpacks and called that lunch.

Kaitlin was kind of haunted by these kids. Despite living right by California's "salad bowl"—an expanse of lush croplands in California's central valley, teeming with greens—their Los Angeles neighborhood was a "food desert." Nothing fresh or leafy could be found for miles around, which is often the case in low-income areas. Seeing the carrot pulp getting tossed, Kaitlin was overcome by the disparities of our split society. Some people have such abundance that they can take just the tiny golden drips of juice from a sack of carrots and toss out the nutritious rest, while other people go completely without.

Equally distressing, in urban areas like Los Angeles, where she lived, just around 2 percent of the high volume of food waste gets composted. Most goes to a landfill, becoming a stew ideal for throwing off heat-trapping methane gas that then seeps out into the atmosphere. In just one week, a single juicery can add thousands of pounds of fruit and veggie byproduct to a landfill. That's not all that goes to waste, either. How about the fresh water to grow the bunch of carrots or kale? Just thinking about all this fallout sends Kaitlin spiraling into "eco-depression"—her term—on the regular.

Just thinking about all this fallout sends Kaitlin spiraling into "eco-depression"—her term—on the regular.

The USC senior started obsessing over finding a constructive use for the produce leftovers, a way that all that goodness might end up in her school kids' tummies. She was convinced people could change their eating habits and develop a taste for healthy foods—she had. "I hated vegetables growing up. My favorite food was filet mignon," she said. Her Chicago meat-and-potato ways are a vague memory. Now she's vegan, she drives an electric car, she installed a bidet in her bathroom (no TP needed), she dresses in secondhand clothes only. . . .

Soon she hatched an idea.

She made a few calls to local juice joints. In less than an hour, Kaitlin had three "suppliers"—stores thrilled to offload their juicing waste pile. She bought a giant Tupperware container at Target, and then drove around doing collections. She then brought her piled-high tub back to the group house where she was living with seven roommates. Pretty soon she would be collecting three hundred pounds of pulp a week—and buying a bunch of much bigger tubs.

Fresh veggie and fruit remains rot quickly, so she had to hurry and cook them all as fast as possible. Freezing could also buy time, but her freezer was just too small. Luckily, her roommates were ready to devour plates piled high with baked goods, for the price of feedback. They even ate her weird beet brownies and carrot-kale cookies. Sometimes her concoctions were full-on health-foodie, like green flax seed crackers. She reached out to a few chefs for advice on recipes, but the ones she found were as enthused as rocks. "They'd say, 'Yeah, I don't think it's going to be possible to stuff veggies in all these things and have them taste good,'" she recalled.

She reached out to a few chefs for advice on recipes, but the ones she found were as enthused as rocks.

Kaitlin kept trying. A few afternoons of hobby baking evolved into renting time in a commercial kitchen, and spending entire weekends dehydrating pulp. She figured out that her best option was to dry out all the material immediately and then grind it into a flour-like powder. That would then be her baking base. "You sure you'd rather be shoulder-deep in kale stems than out Saturday night with us?" her friends asked. "You don't get your college senior year back," they harangued. But she never thought about what she was missing—she had never felt happier. Bliss was buying her first drying machine with the $7,000 in grant money she applied for and got from USC. "I thought I could get a big commercial dehydrator but I could only afford the home model. The money never goes as far as you think it will," she said.

She was mixing her veggie pulp into all kinds of foods. The stuff that was catching on was granola in flavors like beet-red velvet cacao and carrot spice. She actually made the first crunchy bits that sparked the idea for granola by accident, when she charred a pan of veggie brownies. Her roommates said, "More like this!" So she overcooked another panful. She started selling the granola at farmers' markets and a few specialty groceries. She still marvels that anyone bought the "pretty gnarly" stuff. She wasn't just stirring in two spoonfuls of pulp so she could market that she was reusing food waste. In all products, she insists that the very first ingredient—meaning the largest quantity—in her goods be veggies or fruit. "If not, then why am I doing it?" she said.

In the summer of 2019, Kaitlin and Pulp Pantry had a breakout event. She was chosen from among four hundred applicants to be part of Target's first-ever Gen Z business incubator program. A few months before, she had gotten excited about tortilla chips, and she planned to devote this concentrated work time at the incubator to developing those. She flew out to Target headquarters in Minneapolis for eight weeks, where a dozen or so mentors helped her with every aspect of her business.

Even after she returned home, Target was a godsend. As she was gearing up for the first major manufacturing run of the new Pulp Chips, her main Target mentor, who was helpfully a food scientist, came out to LA to coach her through the momentous occasion. "It was scary," she said about laying down the cash to make seven thousand bags of chips from celery and kale remains. Chips she had no idea if anyone would want.

She mailed samples off to all her new Target friends, including the chain's buyer for tortilla chips, who, little did Kaitlin know, had just been made a senior sourcing manager. She fell backward onto her bed when he called to say he wanted to bring Pulp Chips into four hundred stores for a two-month trial. "Definitely pretty surreal," she said. Ultimately, the pandemic delayed the trial. But instead of a bust, the misfortune became a boon. He quickly decided to skip the test run altogether and give Pulp Chips permanent shelf space beginning in fall 2021.

Breaking into Whole Foods soon after was also thrilling. Not surprisingly, they were keen to take Pulp Chips—upcycled foods was among their predicted Top 10 Food Trends for 2021. Kaitlin is now regularly doing manufacturing runs of twenty-five thousand bags a pop, using up ten thousand pounds of waste.

But chips are far from her endgame. Visions of pulp-enriched cereal, pastry crust, baking mixes, and dips all thrill her. "We want to be in every supermarket aisle," she said.

She has no delusions that keeping juicing pulp out of landfills will make a useful dent in our planetary climate emergency. But what she believes she can do is help change culture. Small sustainability hacks influence people. Finding chips created to recycle food waste might spark a plea to your school principal to ban single-use plastics on campus. Or incite a bet on how many days a week your family could stand going meatless. Maybe some Pulp Chips fan gets inspired enough to open her own zero-waste restaurant. "We can't really quantify how our everyday rebellious acts lead to social change," Kaitlin said. "But three years ago, no one was talking about upcycling. Now it's everywhere."

"We can't really quantify how our everyday rebellious acts lead to social change. But three years ago, no one was talking about upcycling. Now it's everywhere."

But Kaitlin is not naive. She knows that being "green" only boosts the appeal if the chips can go head-to-head with Doritos. "You need [to win over] people who are the junk food eaters."

FACT: Over 20 percent of waste in municipal landfills is food, according to US EPA data.

10 Must-Watch Documentaries . . .
Because One Film Spurred Some
of These Women to Action

Three women in this book say a single film made them go green.
They all cite seeing *An Inconvenient Truth,* Al Gore's dry but scary
documentary raising the alarm about global warming, as the epiph-
any moment when they devoted themselves to saving the planet.
So, if a single documentary produced Beautycounter, Pulp Pantry,
and more, then it's time to cut the lights and roll some film. What
about starting a film group instead of a book group, watching and
then discussing? Here's a great list to help you get started:

1. *Artifishal*

2. *Blackfish*

3. *The Cove*

4. *Food, Inc.*

5. *Forks over Knives*

6. *I Am Greta*

7. *An Inconvenient Truth*

8. *An Inconvenient Sequel*

9. *The Island President*

10. *My Octopus Teacher*

11. *No Impact Man*

12. *The Cove*

13. *Who Killed the Electric Car?*

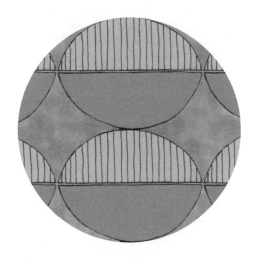

Rhea Mazumdar Singhal

Founder and Chief Executive Officer of

Ecoware

Fighting the great garbage apocalypse

I AM ODDLY GOOD AT: making friends with strangers

I AM ODDLY BAD AT: singing

MY GREATEST FEAR: all chocolate runs out in the house

A GUILTY PLEASURE: fine wine

THE TRAIT I MOST DEPLORE IN MYSELF: inability to say no

AN OCCASION WHEN I LIE: to get my kids to eat their veggies

MY FAVORITE SNACK: Cheetos

In 2009, Rhea Mazumdar Singhal finally moved home to India after twenty-eight years away. Just envisioning of a new life in Delhi tingled all her senses: thinking about tangy red curries, the strum of a sitar, bright orange marigolds, and—oh, flash-fried chapati. She could practically taste the flatbread, squishy and oily on her tongue. . . .

But the ride from the airport through the city was heartbreaking and, frankly, terrifying. All around her, choking the brain, was trash. Flotillas of Styrofoam on dirt-brown waterways. Take-out containers spilling out of trash cans. Plastic bags clinging to tree limbs like leaves. Just beyond the city, a garbage mountain as tall as the Taj Mahal for real.

Rhea was sure that the entirety of her fair Delhi was about to be subsumed by garbage, and neighboring Kolkata next, and before long, all 1.3 billion India inhabitants would be suffocating beneath a gargantuan, rat-infested heap.

A welcome home, this was not.

But this was India's new reality. Massive population + a new convenience culture + extensive poverty + 26,000 tons of plastic coming off production lines daily = the garbage apocalypse. Worse, in Indian cities, there is no sorting or recycling of waste. Seventy percent of plastic is simply tossed, frequently right into the street. "Nobody even knew what 'biodegradable' or 'compostable' meant," she said.

Rhea, who is trained as a pharmacologist and is thus an expert in understanding chemical compounds and how they interact, had seen the scientific studies linking certain plastics to disease. She'd spent most of her twenties in London working for pharmaceutical giant Pfizer, selling and marketing drugs, including for cancer. "Put hot food on a plastic plate, and that plastic melts a bit and toxins leach out into the food. People talk about healthy eating, but they never talk about what they are eating out of or on," she said.

Worse still, many plastics last for two and a half centuries. Those take-out clamshells, once filled with delicious sag paneer, would be around when her kids (which, at that point, she didn't even have) had kids, and their kids had kids, and those kids had kids, and those kids grew up. This boggled her mind. And the Ganges, India's largest river, was second only to China's Yangtze in sweeping plastics into our oceans.

Immediately, Rhea began brainstorming a way out of this destiny. She'd just quit her job at Pfizer, so there was plenty of time to think and investigate. As Rhea saw it, India's only hope was to outpace plastic, replacing the country's bottomless hunger for plastic plates, forks, bottles, and take-out containers with something better and truly disposable. Translated: whatever went up against plastic needed to decompose in less than two hundred years, and preferably in less than two months.

Her research led her, conveniently, to her father-in-law's place of work, a sugarcane refinery in the Delhi area, where the sugar we all know and love is literally wrung out of cane stalks, leaving behind mounds of stringy, decomposing plant fibers. Those fibers, a byproduct called bagasse, have found their way into animal feed and biofuel, but they're just as often burned, producing a putrid smoke that contributes to pollution.

Rhea had another plan for the bagasse. She'd read that in China and Taiwan, engineers were turning it into biodegradable "paper" products. She took a trip around Asia to see for herself. She wondered aloud as she wandered the factories: Could this bagasse, this readily accessible stuff that her father-in-law, in fact, had in excess by the boatload, be the answer to her quest? Could it become meal trays, plates, forks, and take-out containers? Yes, the engineers in Asia said.

Task number one was deciding which products to make first. Back in India, she wandered around Chandni Chowk, Delhi's oldest wholesale bazaar, in search of answers. She found the aisle selling India's most popular disposable plates, bowls, and cups and bought a set. She then sent the items to a factory in Dehra Dun and said, essentially, "Use bagasse to make an identical set."

To make them, the manufacturing plant used a process much like making papier-mâché. Did you ever soak newspaper strips in water and glue until the strips broke down into slop, smother that onto a balloon, let it dry, and make a mask out of it? Same concept. The bagasse is soaked until it becomes oatmeal-consistency mush. This is fed through pipes into a machine and then a mold. Each dinnerware item has its own mold, dotted with tiny holes. Air is then pulled through the molds, powerfully enough to create massive suction, which forces the pulp to stick to the mold. High heat and pressure then basically bake the material into a sturdy product.

Instead of in two hundred forty years, if her dinnerware were buried, it would turn back into soil in ninety days.

Instead of in two hundred forty years, if her dinnerware were buried, it would turn back into soil in ninety days.

She brought that first set of samples back to Chandni Chowk to show the salespeople and ask for their vote of confidence. "Ye nahin chalega medam," they said. Translation: "Madam, this will not work."

She went ahead and molded an entire line of Ecoware anyway.

Instead of converting one person at a time, she decided to attack big accounts. In 2010, her first target was the Commonwealth Games, a massive multi-sport athletic competition involving all the countries that were once territories of the British Empire. The organizers of the event, held in four stadiums across India and a converted "athletes' village," had announced their plan for an environmentally sustainable event. Rhea knew what that meant: Ecoware for all to-go food containers, and disposable plates and cutlery. She pursued the Games' management until they couldn't say no.

Indian Railways fell for Ecoware next, and soon a portion of its 8.4 billion passengers were receiving to-go meals in Ecoware boxes and on Ecoware trays instead of the usual aluminum. "The railways is so big that no one [company] could supply the entire thing," she said. After that, the fast food chain stores Subway and Cinnabon. Then J.P. Morgan and Goldman Sachs in India converted their corporate cafeterias to Ecoware. "Any place that produces and sells food is a potential customer," Rhea says.

Today Rhea's problem is too much interest in her products. "Even if we have three or four more factories, we won't be able to meet the massive demand." Her distribution reaches as far as Sri Lanka and South America. And the COVID-19 pandemic only increased business. Suddenly, single-use, noncontaminating dinnerware was critically needed. And while she was talking to hospitals about their future plastic-free cafeterias, she nudged them to consider dropping other disposable plastics that could be replaced by Ecoware. Like bedpans and urine bottles.

As she increases the volume of Ecoware, she gets better prices from manufacturers and distributors, which drives the unit price of her goods down. That might sound like a bad thing for a business—charging less—but it's actually brilliant. Because—don't forget—to beat plastic, to sideline it forever, Ecoware has to cost less. A company deciding between the two has to be able to say, "Choosing the green option will save me money." When Rhea started Ecoware, her customers could not say that. They paid 50 percent more for her product than they would have for plastic. Those customers could afford the loss, or they placed the environment above profits. Today, Ecoware costs about 15 percent more than plastic—and the number keeps falling. "We are really close to flattening that gap," she said. "Our next big growth will bring us on par with plastic." That is essential for mass adoption.

While that gap flattens, Ecoware has begun work on a line of packaging—remaking Styrofoam to ship wine is first up.

Moving fifty million people off single-use plastic has made Rhea a hero in India. On International Women's Day in 2019, looking regal in her gold-accented sari, she walked the red carpet to its end, then stood face to face with President Ram Nath Kovind. From him she received the highest civilian honor for a woman in India, the Nari Shakti Puraskar (Woman Power Award). As she should have.

> **FACT:** Sugarcane stalks are just one of many agricultural products being turned into fast-biodegrading dishware. Bamboo, palm leaves, and starch from potatoes, corn, and wheat are all becoming plates, bowls, and utensils.

Komal Ahmad

Founder of

Copia

Solving world hunger and
food waste, one sandwich at a time

I AM ODDLY GOOD AT: pickleball

I AM ODDLY BAD AT: my running form (My family tells me I run like Phoebe from *Friends.*)

MY GREATEST FEAR: not fulfilling my potential

THE TRAIT I MOST DEPLORE IN MYSELF: self-doubt

AN OCCASION WHEN I LIE: whenever people ask me if their newborns are cute

A WORD OR PHRASE I MOST OVERUSE: "bro"

A HABIT I'M TRYING TO GIVE UP: procrastination

SOMETHING I USED TO DO BEFORE I REALIZED HOW BAD IT WAS FOR THE ENVIRONMENT: toss take-out containers after one use—now I reuse as Tupperware

Komal Ahmad is out to solve "the World's Dumbest Problem."

She noticed it for the first time on a lovely fall day in 2011. She was twenty-one years old, a senior at UC Berkeley, and hungry. She'd risen early to exercise with fellow Reserve Officers' Training Corps (ROTC) cadets and then had attended back-to-back classes. With this schedule, she was always hungry. That day, as she turned into a favorite café, she locked eyes with a disheveled man leaning against a parking meter. Everything about his stance suggested he was in need. Rather than pass him a wrinkled five-dollar bill, she asked if he would join her for lunch—a sandwich on her.

She learned that he had not eaten in three days. He was just back from his second tour in Iraq and was still waiting for his veteran benefits to kick in. Komal was the first person in her family to do a stint in the military, and the story and the man stunned her. He'd defended his country and was now begging on the street? What was more insane was that, just across the street, a campus dining hall was tossing bags of perfectly good, excess food.

FACT: One-third of all food produced in the world is wasted or lost, according to the Food and Agriculture Organization of the United Nations.

FACT: If food waste were a country, it would be the third-largest emitter of greenhouse gases in the world, after the US and China, according to the United Nations Environment Program. Many environmental experts cite eliminating food waste among their top action items for addressing climate change.

FACT: Fifty-five million people go hungry every day in America (one in six in the population), according to the USDA.

These three facts add up to the World's Dumbest Problem.

That fall day Komal decided to do something about it. She knew there was a logistical way to solve the World's Dumbest Problem. She just had to find organizations with too much food and connect them to places with too little. She needed to become a food matchmaker.

She started with the UC Berkeley dining halls. She'd been told that the halls' food could not be donated due to liability concerns (i.e., if the food made someone sick, the school might be sued). But a little research dispelled that myth. New laws had been passed that made giving away food permissible and legally safe.

She started to put up signs, introduce herself to food managers all over town, talk up her plan. It was a slow process. Throwing food away is easier than dealing with it in a better way, and organizations were resistant to change. But then, when she was sitting in class one afternoon, her cell phone rang. She rushed outside to take the call. It was one of the many local food managers she had contacted.

"We have five hundred extra gourmet sandwiches to donate. You want them?" the caller asked.

Komal was ecstatic. When her biology lecture ended, she bolted out the door to find the nearest Zipcar pickup spot. While driving, she made calls to shelters, soup kitchens, and after-school programs to see who most needed the sandwiches. The responses were discouraging, and more discouraging. One-third of her calls weren't even answered. Most said no in one way or another. "We aren't authorized to take donations." . . . "We just had our food delivery." . . . "Sorry. We only distribute groceries."

It's harder to give away a sandwich than you might think.

It's harder to give away a sandwich than you might think.

Finally, though, she got a yes. "We are thrilled by your offer. We can take ten sandwiches." Lovely. Ten down. Only four hundred ninety more to go.

Still, that day an organization was born—Feeding Forward.

Almost every day after was like that first one: exhilarating, exhausting, frustrating. She was a one-woman show—writing grants, packing meals, reaching out to everyone, driving food around, paying herself nothing. Three years in, despite receiving kudos from the Clinton Global Initiative and several student awards, she felt completely burnt out.

She decided she needed stability. Predictability. Rent money. She was sick of fundraising. Her impeccable academic record allowed her to quickly land a job at Google. "Account Technology Strategist" sounded important. Her parents were overjoyed. They were immigrants who had left Pakistan for a better life for their children when Komal was two. They had very specific ideas about possible careers. "I had four options. Doctor, lawyer, engineer, or complete failure," she said, snickering.

But within days, her spiffy title had lost its sheen. She was a human receptacle for complaints. All day, she fielded calls from incensed small-business owners. "They told me how much they hated our service," she said. Her job was to answer as many calls as possible, as quickly as possible, and get people off the phone in as few minutes as possible. "These were not my kind of metrics," she said.

Annoyance oozed out of her every cell. She acted as dispassionately as she felt, and her performance reflected that. Rather unceremoniously, she was fired. For an achiever like Komal, this was devastating. "My life hit rock bottom. I had graduated from UC Berkeley with honors, and I had been fired from an entry-level job answering phones." She even hid the news from her father for years, and only shared the truth later in a graduation speech she gave at California Polytechnic State Institute in 2017, which he attended. "Sorry, Dad," she offered wryly that day from the podium.

Looking back, she could see that this firing was her life's pivotal moment. When she hit bottom, she bounced.

Immediately she dove back into the World's Dumbest Problem. But this time, she would take a new tack. No more scrappy nonprofit, begging for dollars. Copia, her new company, would be a money-making Match.com for meals. It would demonstrate the economic genius of playing middleman. She would charge a subscription fee to handle all the leftover food from corporations, large venues like stadiums, and mass events like the Super Bowl, saving them the hassle and the guilt of wasted meals. Part of the service would be providing data to help businesses predict their food needs more accurately up front, to avoid excess and save money. And those food donors would get a tax break. Meanwhile, organizations that needed meal donations would create online profiles with their needs and preferences.

Added genius: by partnering with DoorDash and Postmates, two national delivery organizations, Copia expanded its business to all fifty states. By 2016, Komal was getting food picked up and delivered in twenty-six minutes, on average. "Hunger is a logistics problem," Komal is always repeating.

"Hunger is a logistics problem."

The process of using technology to connect the food rich with the food poor is still going like gangbusters. On Oscar night 2017, Copia recovered leftovers from the Vanity Fair after-party and delivered the food to the LA LGBT Center and other organizations in LA. In 2019, when the Raiders took on the 49ers for a Bay Area Super Bowl, Copia fed leftover stadium food—pulled pork and lobster rolls—to forty-one thousand people over two days. Several European governments have reached out to Copia to help feed hundreds of thousands of Syrian refugees.

The pandemic has made Komal's work even more critical. Hunger is predominantly hitting women, children, and people of color. Copia has reduced their rates for food pickup. They have new partners, like hospitals, which have excess for giveaway.

The pandemic also triggered Komal to think globally. The interconnectedness of the world's people, juxtaposed with the chasm between rich and poor, hit her deeply as she watched COVID-19 rage. She wondered, "Could my matchmaking model translate to other critical resources where some have too much, and others too little?" She was so intrigued by this wider lens that in early 2021, Komal decided to find out. She passed the Copia torch to her executive team. Now she's planning to step onto the world stage, by founding a new venture to go even bigger with this approach.

But her heart will always stay firmly tethered to her roots. In the University of California system, which includes her alma mater, UC Berkeley, 44 percent of undergraduates worry about having enough to eat, a 2020 UC Regents report found. They don't need a degree to understand the World's Dumbest Problem.

> **FACT:** Food waste is the most prevalent form of waste in American landfills, according to the US EPA.

FACT: Roughly one-third of food produced for human consumption is lost or wasted globally, which amounts to about 1.3 billion tons per year, UNFAO reports.

How to Not Walk Right Past a Problem

1. Act right then and there. If you see a way to help in the moment, do it. You never know where the action will lead. If Komal had never invited the veteran for a sandwich, Copia would not exist.

2. Start locally. Komal's first step in fighting food waste was walking directly across the street to her university dining hall and asking how they handled leftover food, which resulted in helping the school create a donation program. Before you launch a national organization, try fixing the problem in your house, your school, your job, your town.

3. Take personal responsibility. When you pass an office building lit up like a Christmas tree at nine p.m., or get unnecessary plastic utensils with your pizza takeout, do something. Stop in at the restaurant or building and speak to the manager. When the thought "Someone has got to stop this" pops into your brain, think, "Oh, that someone is me."

4. Don't reinvent the wheel. Very likely, there is already a smart organization working to address the problem you want to fix. Can you volunteer to work with them? Lord knows the world does not need more organizations. . . . See if you can work with one that already exists.

5. Develop relationships. People solve problems. If you want to get your school to go meatless on Mondays, get to know your cafeteria manager and other menu decision-makers. They are more likely to be receptive to your idea if you are a friendly, recognizable face.

6. Know your facts cold. If your friends keep buying cheap, trendy rompers and floral miniskirts at H&M and Topshop, be ready with a litany of ugly stats to set their minds spinning. That, way more than chastising, will convince them to change.

Nicole Bassett

Cofounder of

the Renewal Workshop

Giving clothing nine lives

I AM ODDLY GOOD AT: puzzles

I AM ODDLY BAD AT: remembering any lyrics to a song, and yet I still try to sing while mumbling what I think are the words

MY GREATEST FEAR: drowning

THE TRAIT I MOST DEPLORE IN MYSELF: that I struggle with saying no, therefore creating more work for myself

AN OCCASION WHEN I LIE: saying I am fine when I am not

A WORD OR PHRASE I MOST OVERUSE: "honestly"

A HABIT I'M TRYING TO GIVE UP: LOL, I have given up trying to give up habits. I am resigned. I am who I am.

MY FAVORITE SNACK: I love snacks so much . . . toffee-covered peanuts, vegan cheese puffs, Swedish fish, popcorn, chips . . . ahhhh.

SOMETHING I USED TO DO BEFORE I REALIZED HOW BAD IT WAS FOR THE ENVIRONMENT: eat meat

A sea of black yoga pants started it. Nicole Bassett was on a routine factory visit in Shenzhen, China, for her job at sportswear brand Prana, staring out across enough stretchy cropped pairs to outfit every Ashtanga devotee west of the Mississippi. And this was just one room of one manufacturing facility on one day. . . .

The thought scrambled her brain: Where will these go after they've done their last sun salutation?

In America, we toss out clothes faster than we finish a bottle of ketchup. Six months (on average) is all the airtime we grant our fashions, and, boom, we trash them. Polyester, the fabric that makes yoga pants so shapely (and can cause a mortifying camel toe), is among the worst fabrics because it can't be recycled, so it sticks around forever in a landfill.

In America, we toss out clothes faster than we finish a bottle of ketchup.

Most alarming, Nicole could see no promised land where clothing manufacturers would suddenly slow down production because consumers are buying less. "We measure success by one metric alone: profits. Profits over planet. Profits over people. We are using a mindset that is two hundred thirty years old. We still think the only way to grow more revenue is to sell more stuff. To do this means making more and more and more."

Even before she had her yoga pants meltdown in 2014, Nicole had been a leader in the apparel sustainability movement for nearly a decade. Her entrée had been through a summer internship at Patagonia, at age twenty-six, between her two years of graduate school in environmental studies. When she finished school, she was hired as a full-time employee in Patagonia's social responsibility department. Four years later, Prana hired her to be their first-ever director of sustainability. In these roles, she got rid of routine plastic bag use in shipping, launched a supply chain transparency website, targeted new materials to reduce the environmental impact of products, and pushed for more environmentally friendly supply chain practices. But staring at that black polyester mountain, her efforts to date were starting to feel like trying to clear a ski slope by eating mouthfuls of snow.

Every cell in her body was fritzing. . . . Forget baby steps! Business had to transform immediately. The only hope for humanity was for us to adopt a new ethos of use, repair, use some more, recycle into something new.

If yoga pants are basically indestructible, they should serve owners serially. When one hot yoga devotee feels done with the pair, they pass them on. The goal must become extending a product's utility for as long as possible. Her mind was whirring. . . . How would you do this? What would make revitalizing old stuff thrilling?

If yoga pants are basically indestructible, they should serve owners serially. When one hot yoga devotee feels done with the pair, they pass them on.

Following this line of thought, Nicole hatched a concept for an entirely new kind of company. She called it the Renewal Workshop.

The Renewal Workshop would be the clothing equivalent of a *Queer Eye* home makeover, giving apparel new life. Very importantly, Nicole would prove not just the eco value of this approach but the mega cash value. Her company would produce big new profits all while producing zero new stuff. Just as Rent the Runway made sharing clothes trendy, the Renewal Workshop would make revived oldies a badge of honor.

Nicole was uniquely poised to recognize and fix this problem. She'd been brought up to make more with less. She was born in northern British Columbia, where her mid-1970s hippie parents had moved to "live off the land." In their tiny town of Smithers, sharing was essential. Trading a cow for a neighbor's pig was the way of life. This was the territory of the Wet'suwet'en people; their deep connection to the earth would influence newcomers like Nicole.

Straight out of an undergraduate film major at Simon Fraser University, she went to work for the Discovery Channel, editing *Daily Planet,* a documentary series profiling "green" innovators. One episode she worked on explored biodegradable coffins made from grass; another spotlighted Ford Motor Company's effort to detoxify waste sites and install green roofs on corporate buildings. These stories shifted her thinking. "I recognized, 'Oh wow, businesses don't have to be evil. Business is the way to fix big problems.'" The idea lodged deep inside her.

Fast-forward to the launch of the Renewal Workshop in 2015. Her concept, simply put, was a high-throughput fix-it shop. For a fee, her team would take retailers' castaways—the lipstick-stained tank from a dressing room mishap, skinny jeans with a belt loop hanging loose because of a production snafu—repair them, and, voila, put the clothes back into circulation. Between 1 and 3 percent of retail products qualify as damaged. So, for every fifty thousand items a company produces, five hundred to fifteen hundred go to the reject pile. The Renewal Workshop's research found that 82 percent of what brands consider waste can be renewed and resold. That was the stuff Nicole had her eye on.

Nicole began by partnering with a handful of outdoor brands—Prana,

Ibex, Mountain Khakis, and Toad&Co. "Basically, it was just me calling my industry friends," she admitted.

The Renewal Workshop relies heavily on its sewing techs, or "surgeons," as Nicole calls them. "These are the most valuable humans in our company." They rejigger zippers, fix snaps, make holes and snags disappear.

For stains, Nicole invested many thousands of dollars in a high-tech laundry machine the size of a one-car garage. The machine's dry-cleaning method kills microbes, removes hair and body oils, plus—bonus—needs no water. Everything, from puffer jackets to white jeans, emerges squeaky clean.

As magical as the sew techs and laundry machine are, not everything can be revived. The un-fixables get sorted by fabric type. Those that are pure—100 percent cotton or wool or silk—are sent away to be broken down into fibers and spun into new thread or yarn, and then new garments. For fabric blends, which can't be recycled but make up most apparel, the ugly ducklings are shredded and sold as car-seat and other kinds of stuffing.

In other words, nothing escapes Nicole's sorters, because the alternative—tossing—means filling up landfills or burning the clothes and polluting the air with toxic chemicals. . . .

A memorable flub occurred when Renewal first expanded overseas, partnering with fast-fashion giant H&M's sub-brand COS. Hundreds of boxes, each stuffed with thousands of damaged items, started arriving at Renewal's Oregon headquarters. What Nicole had not anticipated is that every single item in every single box they received required an extensive customs form used for imports. One by one, Renewal employees had to document every sweater, pair of sweatpants, and sock pair on its own lengthy slip. Not surprisingly, Renewal has now opened its first workshop in Europe, so they are freed from this bureaucratic form-filling nightmare.

In 2018, Nicole helped the North Face—which was shedding a quarter million "unsalable" units annually—develop a line called North Face Renewed, basically a partnership with the Renewal Workshop. The North Face designers trained with the Renewal Workshop's repair sharks to perfect the tools of the trade. Like the North Face, most of the brands Nicole has helped want to manage their own resale line partnering with the Renewal Workshop to get their products into tip-top shape to be resold, and then taking back over. Pearl Izumi, Prana, Toad&Co, Timbuk2, Carhartt, and even Pottery Barn, which has pillows, towels, and other soft goods that get damaged and can benefit from rehabilitation, have all joined up, and the Renewal Workshop is on target to keep a million pounds of apparel and home goods out of landfills by 2025. Each spiffed-up item gets a tag sewn in, indicating that it has been "renewed."

There is a term for the ideal that Nicole is pioneering: a circular system. She is striving to help clothing act more like trees. Trees live by a circular system. Their leaves grab CO_2 from the atmosphere and, with energy from the sun, make food for the tree. "Leaves fall off in winter, but that is not litter. They make nutrients, which feed the tree, which grows new leaves, and on and on," she said.

> **FACT:** The number of garments produced every year has doubled since 2000, now exceeding 100 billion, a 2016 McKinsey & Co. report states.

> **FACT:** As a whole, the world's citizens acquire some 80 billion items of clothing each year. Each piece will be worn, on average, just seven times before getting tossed, according to British charity Barnado's.

FACT: When you order those jean cutoff shorts in multiple sizes to get the right bum fit and send back the rejects, there's a good chance those go to landfill. Many retailers throw away a shocking 25 percent of their returned items, return logistics company Otoro reports.

FACT: British luxury brand Burberry (think plaid-lined trench coats) destroyed $36.8 million worth of its own merchandise in 2017. The company admitted in its 2018 annual report that demolishing goods was just part of its strategy to preserve its reputation of exclusivity.

Go For Slow Fashion

The clothing resale market is humming as more people understand the evils of fast fashion. Secondhand shopping can also be more game than chore—the thrill of the hunt for finds. You will be spared the embarrassment of stepping into school beside two others wearing the same Zara crochet crop top you are. Plus, already-worn jeans = comfier. Try these ideas for better swapping, thrifting, and reselling:

SWAP MEET

Face it, we get sick of our clothes. But no need to rush out and buy new. Throw a swap party. Invite a crowd to ensure size and style variety. When friends arrive with their armloads, set up a "shop" with clothes on hangers, and outfits accessorized. Try organizing by color for a unique boutique-y feel. Remind everyone to bring their done-with clutches, jewelry, and phone cases, because these don't require just the right fit, which increases the chance that all can leave with something great. You could cap the night with a fashion show of swapped items, with prizes for taking the biggest fashion risk. Set some ground rules before swapping so the scene doesn't turn into a grab fest. Figure out beforehand where you'll donate the items nobody takes.

THRIFTING

Finding great items at thrift stores is a skill like playing tennis or ukulele—the more you "play," the better you get. There is an art to learn, like leaving Saturday to the hordes and going Wednesday after school instead, or asking the manager which day restocking happens so you can plan your visits to coincide. Go when you feel relaxed and have time to be patient. The amazing leather mini will inevitably be on the rack that is so stuffed, you can barely move the clothes, so take your time. Don't hit too many stores in a day. You'll do better digging deep for the gems.

RESELLING

It stinks that most clothes are being tossed within six months of purchase. Those wide-leg red jeans were a bad fashion miss for you, but someone else covets them. Selling clothes online, once you get the hang of it, is simple, and the cash is nice, too. For reselling and buying secondhand, check Depop. Twenty-one million teens around the world are downloading this app and uploading their clothes pics. Other options: Asos Marketplace, eBay, Poshmark, the RealReal, ThredUp. Another idea: Crossroads Trading will send you a bag with a prepaid shipping label so you can mail in your has-beens for them to sell, and they'll send you a check or store credit. Unfortunately, the trendiness of some of these apps is driving prices up on the sites. This gentrifying of the secondhand clothing market squeezes those who depend on cheap resale finds. So keep in mind that while wearing used clothing is better than supporting new fast fashion, the most sustainable practice is to always ask yourself, Do I really need this? and resist the urge when the answer, as it often is, is no.

Lindsay Stradley

Cofounder of

Sanergy

Taking toilets where none have gone before

I AM ODDLY GOOD AT: I can find anything. My husband and kids misplace things—I'm the detective called in.

I AM ODDLY BAD AT: Despite my love of sports, I'm just not coordinated.

MY GREATEST FEAR: That we're already too late to successfully green the planet. I don't think we are (or I wouldn't do what I do!), but I fear it.

THE TRAIT I MOST DEPLORE IN MYSELF: When I'm stressed, I'm not kind to those around me. I cut out all nonessentials such as communicating with friends.

MY GREATEST ACHIEVEMENT: two kind, thoughtful, worldly children—still a work in progress

A WORD OR PHRASE I MOST OVERUSE: "impact"

A HABIT I'M TRYING TO GIVE UP: talk less, listen more

SOMETHING I USED TO DO BEFORE I REALIZED HOW BAD IT WAS FOR THE ENVIRONMENT: I loved bacon. My grandmother would cook a whole package with me standing at her side, eating it as fast as she could cook it.

The drive from Boston to the White Mountains takes about three and a half hours. A packed car in August humidity made for some pungent BO but also a certain intimacy—five students, backpacks stuffed with three days' worth of beef jerky and DEET, and all the ambition of newly minted graduate business students beginning orientation at the Massachusetts Institute of Technology (MIT). Quite unexpectedly, the get-acquainted banter veered far from financial analyst war stories. Somehow everyone along was hell-bent on saving the world. First in the car, and then on the trail, they wrestled with how to slash poverty, clean drinking water, and power the developing world.

They couldn't have known this at the time, but this trip, for three of the MIT newbies, would be their life launchpad. Two would end up getting married—Lindsay Stradley and Ani Vallabhaneni. With a third, David Auerbach, they would cross the globe to develop a venture to bring toilets to poor urban settlements. Their inventive approach turned locals into small-business owners plus recycled the human waste into organic fertilizer and animal feed for area farmers, making it the kind of circular enterprise that social scientists swoon over.

By the time the students had returned to campus, they had made a pact to find their world-changing idea and get that concept going. A cool department at MIT is the D-Lab, specializing in multidisciplinary, design-based problem-solving. Lindsay, Ani, and David tried registering for the Development Ventures class in the D-Lab, but only two got slots, and that was just to audit the course. The threesome decided that the two who'd lucked out would be the emissaries, but they would all use the course to develop a real business. The semester's project prompt was to solve a poverty-related problem affecting at least one billion people.

With that requirement, landing on sanitation "was really obvious," Lindsay recalled. According to USAID, over half the world—4.6 billion people—

still lack this basic necessity, have a subpar "pit," or rely on "flying toilets," as Lindsey describes them, going in a plastic or paper bag that they then hurl into the street in the dark of night, as she saw in Kenya and elsewhere. The students ultimately landed on building a better toilet for impoverished urban neighborhoods and schools. Lack of toilets, they discovered, created more of a problem than just feces-strewn streets. Human waste contaminates the environment and water, causing disease, death, and billions of dollars in lost productivity. A lack of private toilets is the top reason schoolgirls drop out when they start having their periods. Public toilets that are a distance from homes become magnets for sexual violence.

A lack of private toilets is the top reason schoolgirls drop out when they start having their periods.

Lindsay was all in on launching a venture to attack this problem. She had a knack for building organizations from scratch. Just before attending MIT, she'd grown Google's very first ad sales unit outside of California, in Michigan, from a five-person experiment to three hundred staffers.

Where she had really honed her start-up mettle was as a math teacher turned school head in New Orleans.

In 2004, just out of Yale undergrad, she joined Teach for America, a program that places college graduates to teach in America's neediest schools. Her post was the New Orleans Center for Science and Math ("or SciHigh, as we'd say"). She created every lesson herself, figuring out the tricky balance of guiding the confused and challenging the gifted. Then, one Friday afternoon, while Lindsay was writing Monday's lesson on her classroom whiteboard, her student Asia popped her head in. "Ms. Stradley.

I think there's going to be a hurricane, so I might not see you Monday." Lindsay was skeptical. But Saturday night, Lindsay went to a bar to hear the popular New Orleans Rebirth Brass Band, and the musicians uncharacteristically didn't show. Then she saw cars in lines circling the block, waiting to get to gas pumps. She jumped into her car and sped home to Atlanta. Two days later, Hurricane Katrina took New Orleans to its knees. Lindsay spent weeks tracking down all her students, tricky with no functional home phones and no school directories to check. Every kid, thankfully, turned up safe.

The damage was mind-boggling. But by late fall, families started returning to the city, desperate to get their kids back to learning. Lindsay and her principal wanted their kids back in school, but their building was leveled. With the city in chaos, the public schools had no plans to reopen. Lindsay and her principal decided that the fast option was to start a brand-new school. Lindsay drove to Baton Rouge, the state capital, to beg Department of Education officials to provide them an intact building in New Orleans. Pickings were slim, but they got access to an elementary school. Oh well. Teens would have to get over mini toilets and knee-high water fountains. By January, New Orleans Charter Science and Mathematics High School was up and running, then the sole school in all of New Orleans. All the sleuthing Lindsay had done to find her kids meant she had a great roster of phone numbers for signing students up. The school was a massive success. Lindsay's skill set now included writing a new organization's charter, hiring staff, building a budget, fundraising—all the functions of starting a business.

The summer after Lindsay's first year of business school, the core toilet team of Lindsay, Ani, and David headed to Nairobi. Ani, an engineer, built two test toilets. Lindsay worked for a nonprofit building schools in poor, high-density areas, as a way to get the lay of the land. "Our initial five toilets we located by those schools. We weren't following," Lindsay explained, referring to the nonprofit. "We were choosing these places for the same reason they were. High need."

Back at school in the fall, the Sanergy team reluctantly entered MIT's annual business-plan competition. This event was beloved "the way other schools love their football," Lindsay said, chuckling. As the Sanergy students saw it, they had no prayer. With all the brainiacs in MIT's best-in-nation engineering, physics, computing, and math departments, a D-Lab social science venture was sunk. Well, Sanergy stopped the streak. Their plan and model toilet were so well conceived, the judges decided that this group might truly start this business, meaning the prize money would go to a real use. Lindsay opened an official Sanergy bank account and deposited the $100,000 check.

The day after graduation, in 2011, Lindsay and her two cofounders moved to Nairobi. They brought a gaggle of undergrads who were up for an adventurous summer job. The whole group of ten stuffed into a small apartment. "It was a bit like *Real World*," Lindsay said. Out back, they built an experimental composting toilet, and poured samples of concrete outhouse bases. They couldn't find the squat platform they needed but figured out a substitute that they imported from a kayak manufacturer in Seattle.

The D-Lab approach had taught them how much good design matters. To determine what "good design" meant for their toilets, they interviewed target users. They had them demonstrate how they would most comfortably be situated on the john (wearing clothes, of course). The feedback showed the importance of features like a hook for your bag, and a mirror. Squatting was preferable to sitting for shared toilets. Amidst all the rusty corrugated metal buildings in Nairobi, a brick structure would signal something safe and permanent. White tile signaled clean. Tile was pricey, so the team tried white epoxy paint. Winner. Separating solid and liquid waste required two holes, but the holes couldn't be so far apart to require scooting to use both.

Sanergy also devised the kind of savvy business model that smarty-pants MIT kids think up. Their clever idea was to sell the toilets as mini-businesses. The owner would charge a small amount for use and be motivated to keep it tidy like their livelihood depended on it. Sanergy workers would circle around picking up the solid waste—the liquid waste just seeps into the ground so doesn't need to be dealt with—and transform it into chemical-free fertilizer and animal feed. Instead of sanitation being a huge cost for governments or individuals, this model flipped that dynamic. Now sanitation was a job, a source of income.

How human poop comes to be animal feed involves an ingenious transformation. There is huge demand for cheap, protein-rich feed in East Africa. Farmers are often forced to import supplies to fill the need, which gets costly; and typically the feed came from dried fish, which are limited in supply. To turn human waste into livestock nourishment, the Sanergy team deploys the black soldier fly. They breed fly eggs in a nursery, then place the larvae on the fecal matter, which the larvae then feed off. Within weeks, the larvae become pupae, which are collected and dried, becoming protein-filled animal feed. The remaining waste from the process is turned into an odorless compost.

But just because these MIT superstars brilliantly applied inventive methods like this one doesn't mean they didn't also screw up royally at times getting their business going. The toilets went on sale on World Toilet Day in 2011—November 19. Lindsay gave her sales pitch a hundred differ-ent ways, but for twenty-five days, zippo sales. Finally, one measly toi-let sold. In December, they sold just one more. Despite a stack of Excel spreadsheets, they had blown it on pricing. Charging 50,000 Kenyan shillings ($500) was too steep. They then partnered with Kiva, a platform that connects small businesses with small lenders. Maybe you've been a Kiva lender, helping a farmer in India buy his goat. . . . That's how it works. Buyers could get the toilet now, pay off the loan over two years. That was a game changer. Come January, they had ten toilet sales.

The November toilet delivery was another fiasco. During installation, the cops showed up. "You got permits?" they asked. Well, Sanergy had met with government officials. They had the required permission, and had signed on the required dotted line . . . they thought. But transactions are not so straightforward in Nairobi. One government official doesn't necessarily alert the others. Arrests were made, and the poor Sanergy staff were hauled to the jailhouse. (They got out fast.)

During installation, the cops showed up. "You got permits?" they asked.

Lindsay continues to roll out toilets. They've now installed over three thousand sky-blue structures resembling old-school phone booths, enabling a hundred thousand Kenyans every day to do their business. And her customer base, which will eventually extend beyond Kenya and perhaps even Africa, is growing daily. This group, the exact target for a Sanergy toilet, is set to double to two billion worldwide by 2030, according to the United Nations (UN). Lindsay is ready. She even supplies toilet paper.

FACT: Today, 700 million urbanites live without proper sanitation, contributing to poor health conditions and heavy pollution, the UN reports.

III

It's Raining Plastic (Literally)

Caroline Danehy

Cofounder and Chief Creative Officer of

Fair Harbor

4,489,222 plastic bottles upcycled
into bathing suits . . .
and they're just getting started

I AM ODDLY GOOD AT: backward running

I AM ODDLY BAD AT: No matter how I try, I just don't have any rhythm.

A GUILTY PLEASURE: catching up on reality TV with a cup of coffee on Saturday morning

THE TRAIT I MOST DEPLORE IN MYSELF: getting anxious

A TIME I'D RATHER NOT REMEMBER: Ninth grade. I was getting recruited to play college lacrosse, but my body had different plans. I was getting stress fractures in my shins and would soon be told by my doctor that I had to stop playing altogether.

MY GREATEST ACHIEVEMENT: Hmm. I'd have to say Forbes 30 Under 30. Since I was young, I've looked at the Forbes list every year and aspired one day that I would be included on it.

IF I COULD CHANGE ONE HUMAN BEHAVIOR TO SAVE THE PLANET: more mindfulness—being aware of what you're consuming, how you're consuming it, where it's going

Caroline Danehy was a vegetarian by age five, nagged others to stop wasting water, and can show you scars from glass cuts she earned cleaning parks as a kid. But raised in the affluent New York suburbs, she was also a clothes horse. At age eleven, still in braces, she began taking the train into Manhattan to attend fashion camp. She had her own style blog, *Cookies Cakes and Cardigans.* Then came high school, where having the right outfit was paramount, no matter how it was sourced, especially boots with big buckles, metallic shoes, and her many "statement pieces." She thought of her high school's hallway as her runway. Weekends were about thrifting (the most sustainable shopping, so a sign of future directions) but were also about lurking around Lincoln Center, tailing anyone who looked like they might have a spare ticket to a Fashion Week event. She scored them more often than not. Once, at a Duckie Brown show, she walked up to a major Macy's exec and handed him her business card. (It read "fashion blogger," naturally.) She and the exec are now doing business together, nearly a decade later. But let's not get ahead of our story.

All through her childhood, Caroline spent her summers on Fire Island, a popular getaway about two hours' drive from her Westchester home, where her family had a beach house. Those were barefoot, coconut-scented-sunscreen days, when she pedaled around on a beater bike. No cars allowed on the island, just little red wagons to transport bags from the ferry. She learned to surf there and lived out most days dressed in a cute bikini and flip-flops, and not much else. The pristine setting burrowed deep into her soul. But the spell was broken when one summer during high school, in 2014, she started noticing plastic trash washing up on the beach.

Enter Jake, her older brother, a junior at Colgate University at the time. He and Caroline were tight. He shared her obsession with Fire Island. The plastic on the beach seriously freaked him out, too. So, at school, he started to research the problem. The stats he found were staggering: World plastic production since 1950 had increased sixtyfold, per Plastics Europe data. Each year, billions of bottles provide one drink in the United States and then get trashed. One million bottles are purchased every minute, National Geographic reports. Ten million tons of plastic end up in the ocean every year, according to Plastic Oceans International. A Cuvier's beaked whale washed up dead in the Philippines with eighty-eight pounds of plastic in its body. Microplastics have been falling from the sky in the Rocky Mountains, evaporated out of the oceans and coming down in rain. By 2050, according to the World Economic Forum, there will be more plastic in the ocean than fish, by weight.

By 2050, according to the World Economic Forum, there will be more plastic in the ocean than fish, by weight.

It was too much. There had to be solutions. Jake began to study emerging technologies that repurpose plastic so that it doesn't go straight to the dump or the ocean. He read about a mill converting plastic bottles into thread, and then weaving that thread into fabric. The fabric on-screen didn't look like the burlap-sack-type fabric he usually associated with "recycled" fibers; this stuff looked cool enough to wear on Fire Island.

He called Caroline, told her everything, and, that day, the teen fashionista merged her clothing passion with her environmental roots.

Unsure where to start, the sibs spent a few days bumbling around Manhattan's garment district with a bit of the fabric, looking for help. After a bunch of door-knocking, they succeeded in convincing a tailor to make them a pair of swim and board shorts to Caroline's very detailed specs.

Then the Danehy pair bought a little more fabric and had a few more shorts made. They named their clothing-line-to-be "Fair Harbor," after the part of Fire Island they loved most.

The next spring, Colgate's entrepreneurship center put on a mock *Shark Tank* competition. Fair Harbor entered. Caroline, still in high school, came for the weekend. Jake's lacrosse team buddies strutted the stage in the prototype threads, while the audience whistled and screamed. The sales pitch: Fair Harbor would be a casual-lifestyle brand making all kinds of recycled clothing, launching with their signature item, surf-ready swim trunks that double as all-day knock-around shorts—literally the staple clothing item anyone near a body of water wears from June to September.

A star-studded panel had come to campus to judge—MC Hammer, Warby Parker's Neil Blumenthal, Jessica Alba of the Honest Company. Jessica, a pioneer in the "green product" movement, was so blown away by what she was seeing that she called one "model" over so she could get her hands on the fabric. "Can those really be soft?" she said. That fabric fondle was something to see, Caroline described with great animation.

The siblings took first prize, $20,000.

With the money, they could finally produce more than two dozen boardshorts at a time. They got a tip about a manufacturing website called Maker's Row that led them to a consultant who helped them locate a Guatemalan factory to make the first five hundred pairs.

That July, they loaded up their car with the new Fair Harbor gear and hit the East Coast beach circuit—Montauk, Sag Harbor, Nantucket, Long Beach Island. They would stash their foldable table in the car trunk, and open shop when they hit the beach. In thirty days, the shorts were sold out. They joke that those first five hundred shorts went to "the 3F's: friends, family, and fools."

Come fall, Caroline followed Jake to Colgate. When they weren't practicing lacrosse together or trading tales of their late-night antics, they planned Fair Harbor—the website's functionality and the Kickstarter campaign.

In 2016, after a year of DIY selling, they felt ready for an official "launch" and threw a bash for one hundred fifty at the trendy rooftop pool and lounge of the Delancey hotel in Manhattan. Jake, sporting his navy Fair Harbor shorts, made the rounds. A few beers into the night, he had to pee—and disaster struck. While he was zipping up his fly, the Velcro closure on his shorts fully detached. He looked more closely. The Velcro had not been sewn on but rather had been glued on. Frick! Glue for a piece of clothing that would be constantly wet? Jake walked back to the pool deck and saw guests lining up to buy boardshorts.

The very next morning, Jake and Caroline sent every purchaser a prepaid return envelope, and a note to send back the shorts. They then vastly overpaid a seamstress to fix every pair—fast—and gave their main factory hell. They doubled down on reviewing and re-reviewing all details. These days, they use Lycra closures—that is, no-fly designs.

The next two summers, their game plan remained the same. Road-trip with the shorts and a table. Hit every beach town from Cape Cod, Massachusetts, to Charleston, South Carolina, giving extra attention to towns where paddleboard or surf competitions were happening. All in all, they held over five hundred beachside trunk shows. Their high-touch approach was intentional. They wanted to know their customers. From one summer to the next, they would check in with them. How did the suit wear? How's the chafe? Did they work to surf in? Lining or no? The siblings spun the feedback into their new styles.

All this time, Fair Harbor's headquarters was still the home where they'd grown up. Every family member helped out. Their parents looked the other way when ten summer interns descended and boldly helped themselves to the family hot tub and grill. "One Friday night, UPS pulled up with eight pallets of boxes." Once they were unloaded and stacked up, there stood a cardboard tower about four Christmas trees tall and three more wide. Still, Mom and Dad didn't blink. In 2019, Caroline and Jake finally got a proper workspace.

That same year, just before Caroline's college graduation, *Forbes* magazine invited her to Israel to their first-ever Forbes Under 30 Global Women's Summit. "I was scared out of my mind," she admits. She was the only college-age attendee. "That's the first environment I've been in where there wasn't one definition of how a business executive looks. The women were quirky and confident. It made a big impression on me," she said.

The male-dominated business world is still making sense of Caroline, however. Sometimes, at investor meetings, men will avoid eye contact with her, focusing their attention on Jake instead. She has every reason to deserve investors' respect and attention. The Fair Harbor website keeps a running tally of how many plastic bottles its factory has shredded into bits, melted down, poured into extruding machines, pulled into thread, and weaved into shorts. The count as of April 2021: 4,289,222. Every pair of shorts repurposes eleven bottles. Last holiday season, choosy J.Crew featured Fair Harbor on its website, and Caroline is now developing a line of Henley T-shirts, as well as women's shirts and soon swimsuits to add to the Fair Harbor brand.

The Fair Harbor website keeps a running tally of how many plastic bottles its factory has weaved into shorts. The count as of April 2021: 4,289,222.

Obviously, turning bottles into wearables isn't Game Over as far as the environmental-waste challenge. The ocean will be spared those bottles, but there is still a pair of boardshorts coming into the world, which could well be stuffed in a landfill tomorrow. To keep Fair Harbor gear out of oceans and trash, Caroline created the Fair Harbor Round Trip Initiative—basically an open invitation to send Fair Harbor your used bathing suits (of any label) to be upcycled—that is, turned into car-seat and pillow stuffing. Fair Harbor even pays for the shipping. And each mailed suit is worth five dollars off the next Fair Harbor purchase (up to twenty-five dollars). Someday, Caroline and Jake want to go totally circular, turning old Fair Harbor wares into new ones.

Caroline feels hopeful. Right before the pandemic, she strolled the New York fabric show, where in a few laps, you learn what is hot industry-wide. "Every vendor had recycled polyester [made from plastic]. This isn't a moment. This isn't a trend. This is a movement," she said.

Conferencing on Zoom from her spare New York City apartment, hair in a tight ponytail, the twenty-three-year-old said she has found her deeper purpose in fashion. "Everyone has their Fair Harbor they want to protect."

FACT: According to Greenpeace, every single piece of plastic ever made still exists. if Leonardo da Vinci had drunk water from a plastic bottle when he was painting the Mona Lisa, that bottle would not have fully decomposed yet.

ORIGIN STORY: In the latter half of the nineteenth century, billiard ball producers recognized they needed a substitute for ivory, which comes from elephant tusks. People were using more than one million pounds of ivory a year, and newspapers warned that elephants were on their way to extinction if this continued. And so the race was on to invent a new material. Voila, plastic was invented.

Trash-Talking the Trashiest Businesses

Social media is a powerful weapon for holding polluters to account. Public shaming can light fires under bums, and force change. What we buy matters, and we can register our vote with our dollars, but mega shifts are going to require that corporations reinvent their bottles and packaging. Here are some ways to use Twitter and Instagram to pressure a move away from single-use plastic:

Tweet the mess: With photos and social media, a standard beach or park cleanup can suddenly have a big impact. After everyone gathers the trash, lay it all out in a designated area and sort everything by brand. The Starbucks cups, tops, sip hole plugs (seriously???) go together. In another pile, every plastic bottle courtesy of PepsiCo, which includes Gatorade, Aquafina, Sierra Mist, and more. (Google to find their full list of sub-brands.) Take a pic of each brand's mound, and tweet it out with something like "Hey, @[brand name], you win 'Worst Polluter of the Day.' Clean it up!" You might even box up all the Starbucks waste and walk it into the nearest store. Tell the manager why you are bringing their trash back.

Make noise: Join Greenpeace in their campaign to pressure large retailers—like Trader Joe's, Target, and Safeway—to reduce the plastic packaging in their stores. When you shop, snap pictures of overly packaged items. Tweet the photos, plus tag the store and the product manufacturer. While you're there, find the manager and make an in-person complaint, too. Do this every time you go to the store.

Pile on: Break Free from Plastic (breakfreefromplastic.org) has a Take Action tab that lists their campaigns, with links to toolkits for jump-starting participation. Learn how to do a plastic audit of school, work, or home. On Instagram at #breakfreefromplastic, you can see examples of efforts all over the world to stop the overuse of plastics. Join the sixty-four thousand others who have jumped onto this bandwagon, by posting photos of plastic trash, or ideas for alternatives, tagged with #breakfreefromplastic.

Saba Gray

Cofounder and Chief Executive Officer of
BioGlitz

Taking the litter out of glitter

I AM ODDLY GOOD AT: being graceful on the ice and a complete klutz off the ice

I AM ODDLY BAD AT: being organized in my home life—like in my closet

I WISH I HAD LEARNED WHEN I WAS YOUNG: more discipline in tasks that aren't the most fun to do (e.g., taxes)

A WORD OR PHRASE I MOST OVERUSE: "honestly"

A HABIT I'M TRYING TO GIVE UP: procrastination—waiting for the deadline pressure to finish

THREE THINGS I WOULD TAKE TO A DESERT ISLAND: glitz, my vintage Dior silk robe, and my dog (a Rhodesian ridgeback and pit bull mix)

SOMETHING I USED TO DO BEFORE I REALIZED HOW BAD IT WAS FOR THE ENVIRONMENT: use single-use toothbrushes

Saba Gray often wears her shiny, dark hair in high pigtails. Her outfits are wild mash-ups—a mod green jumpsuit with seventies hot-pink hoops;

a black-and-red tie-dyed wrap paired with a studded belt. She's gutsy and original—no surprise she was voted Best Dressed at Ballard High School in Louisville, Kentucky. Before she steps out (or online), she always adds a critical finishing touch: glitter. She might paint on a shimmery Wonder Woman–esque eye mask or spray gold and pink stardust across one cheek. She cannot greet the day without glitter.

To think, she used to despise the stuff.

That was back in her figure-skating days, when life was a never-ending series of double-toe-loop jumps and sit-spins in short sequined dresses. The "dance moms" made all the girls dress like adults, and, of course, that meant glitter dusted everywhere to please the judges. It bugged Saba.

It also bugged her when all her friends started showing up at school dressed top to bottom in Limited Too and Urban Outfitters gear. Saba didn't want to look exactly like everyone else, plus her mom would never pay those box-store prices. So, Saba got creative. If she saw an Urban skirt she liked, something decorated in shiny buttons and pins, say, she'd scour secondhand stores for a skirt in a similar cut, then coat every inch with her own collection of bling.

Eventually even the fashion routine at school got tiresome, so she took enough AP classes to satisfy administrators, and graduated from high school a year early. With her babysitting savings, she bought herself a plane ticket to Spain. She did a family stay in Madrid. The well-dressed local women impressed her. "Even walking in the park or running to the corner bodega, they worry about style," she said. She quickly realized how much fashion moved her. Once back home in the US, she chased the feeling.

That meant, instead of college, she headed to New York City, America's fashion capital. It was a rude awakening. Fashion, it turns out, is a pollution nightmare. An internship with a handbag manufacturer revealed the underbelly of leather production, with its worrisome environmental impact from nasty dyes, not to mention methane from all those animals. Not for her. Next, she joined an "incubator" program helping up-and-coming fashion designers looking to launch indie lines with an environmentally sustainable business model. The place was called Manufacture New York. Its goals: save the planet and restore the city's once-vibrant textile industry, which disappeared with the rise of cheap production. This was the place for her. What she learned there as a product developer committed to local and green production affected everything that came next.

First, though, Saba fell in love with glitter. For a young person living in New York, frequenting dance clubs and festivals—glitter took on a whole new meaning. Glitter meant gay pride. Glitter meant self-expression. Glitter meant "subverting traditional beauty standards, rejecting conformity, and blurring gender lines." Saba came to see that "it's not just a shiny thing." Whenever she wore glitter out, people engaged with her differently. A grumpy family on the bus was suddenly all smiles. Before going dancing, she would strap on her fanny pack stuffed with vials of glitter. Then she'd spread the love . . . glitzing everyone she met with her collection of colors.

Glitter meant gay pride. Glitter meant self-expression. Glitter meant "subverting traditional beauty standards, rejecting conformity, and blurring gender lines."

As much as the stuff helped people bond and feel free, Saba knew that the little flecks of plastic were bad news for the environment. They infiltrated water systems and fish tummies and more.

"The more we wore it, the more guilt we felt," said Saba.

But then she had one of her go-my-own-way ideas: "What if I can make glitter eco-safe?"

Saba summoned up the chutzpah to pitch the idea at work. Her boss and mentor at Manufacture New York, Bob Bland (aka Mari Lynn Foulger, cofounder of the Women's March of 2016), immediately perked up. Bob backed Saba instantly. "Do it!" Then she volunteered to help.

In no time, Saba was off on research trips with Bob. First stop: a conventional glitter manufacturer in New Jersey where glitter was made from thin sheets of pressed plastic cut into tiny shapes. It was bad. But it used to be worse, Saba learned. Original glitter was made of shards of glass.

Original glitter was made of shards of glass.

She needed to explore alternatives. She investigated a shiny rock called mica but rejected the option when she discovered it was mined by child slave labor. (See page 16 for more on that. . . .) She explored insect resins and even an edible powder made by recycling methane and feeding it to E. coli. The methane and E. coli powder was then pressed into sheets that look and feel like plastic. But the process was too untested. She needed something that worked NOW.

Undaunted, she continued her hunt, visiting her new buddy in Brooklyn, Rebecca Richards, for a pep talk. Rebecca was an NYU student studying sustainable fashion who regularly cruised the vintage clothes shops in her free time. Saba and Rebecca had met sharing a mirror in a thrift shop and had fallen "instantly in fashion love," Saba recalls. Not surprisingly, Rebecca was totally into Saba's mission to make safer glitter. Actually,

Rebecca wanted to be more than a cheerleader. A business partnership was forged.

Together, they would bring the world BioGlitz, biodegradable glitter.

Biodegradable glitter was originally the brainchild of an Englishman, Ronald Britton, in charge of England's largest art supply business. BioGlitz—founded as "Bioglitter" by Britton—is made from the harvested cellulose of eucalyptus tree leaves. Like for all glitter, the cellulose is turned into plastic-like sheets that are cut into shapes. Color pigment is then added, as well as a minute amount of aluminum for shine— 0.1 percent.

Saba and Rebecca saw the opportunity and leapt. Ronald had no understanding of how this product might be positioned for the fashion market. Saba and Rebecca were all about that. In 2016, the Bioglitter team had plans to be in Malibu, California, and Saba targeted that visit as her chance to woo the Brit. She proposed a partnership wherein she would launch a wholly separate entity, BioGlitz, creating a fashion wing of his company. "I worked for months on my presentation," she said. Saba's passion, smarts, and complementary skills won Ronald over. She and Rebecca would be Ronald's fashion partners, making inroads into new categories, starting with the obvious—makeup. Saba was just twenty-three years old, and became CEO of BioGlitz.

After makeup glitter, Saba jumped into a new category, textile glitter. She wanted sparkly decals on T-shirts, and fabric with embedded glitter.

By the time this book publishes, you may well see BioGlitz in some of fashion's biggest labels—Balenciaga and Yves Saint Laurent, to name two. Saba is careful not to say too much, but she feels that "anything shiny on a garment" in the next few years could be her stuff. Discussions, in fact, are already underway.

"Experimental" and "opportunistic" are two words Saba is not afraid of. She's currently living seven hundred sixty miles from the capital of American fashion, back in Louisville. The situation is counterintuitive, which makes sense, given her independent streak. But the inexpensive city is allowing her to mess with the idea of opening a storefront. The concept (the inspired vision of one of her employees) is a glitter lab where salespeople in white coats help customers mix their own glitter, sip wine, and kibitz with besties. A perfect graduation or bachelorette party location. The concept has gone from dream to reality already. The first store opened in June 2021.

Saba is changing the face—no pun intended—of the sustainability movement. With BioGlitz, she's making the movement downright chic.

FACT: Plastic glitter takes about one thousand years to biodegrade.

FACT: For some time, the US Air Force employed a military strategy using "chaff," essentially glitter but made of aluminum or zinc-coated fibers instead of plastic or eucalyptus, which they released from the back of warplanes to confuse the radar of enemy forces.

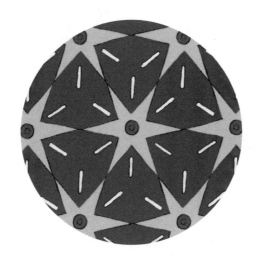

Sarah Paiji Yoo

Cofounder and Chief Executive Officer of

Blueland

Clearing out household plastic

I AM ODDLY GOOD AT: staying calm and optimistic

I AM ODDLY BAD AT: spelling

MY GREATEST FEAR: losing a loved one

A GUILTY PLEASURE: late-night ice cream

THE TRAIT I MOST DEPLORE IN MYSELF: feeling guilty about not doing enough as a mom and CEO

AN OCCASION WHEN I LIE: to my mom—so she won't worry about the small things happening in my life

A TIME I'D RATHER NOT REMEMBER: my father's battle with pancreatic cancer and subsequent passing

I WISH I HAD LEARNED WHEN I WAS YOUNG: to ski

A SMALL LIFE "HACK" I DO TO HELP THE ENVIRONMENT, WHICH YOU COULD DO, TOO: When ordering takeout, ask the restaurant to hold all plastic utensils, condiments, and napkins.

Sarah Paiji Yoo sat staring at her computer, stumped. She had a classic dilemma: "How do I research how to do something that has never been done before?"

All she wanted to do was take one of those unwieldy, curse-when-carrying-it-up-your-apartment-steps, ten-pound jugs of bathroom cleanser and compress it into a tablet the size of two Mentos. Then she wanted the tablet to get plopped into a reusable container filled with tap water, and presto—a cleaning product that provides freedom from back pain, freedom from the plastic jug skyscraper teetering above the garbage bin, freedom from plastic poisoning the planet and her new baby boy.

But it was just a fantasy. She had no background in manufacturing. No experience with research and development (aka R&D). She had not touched a chemistry beaker since college. Or was it high school?

She had not touched a chemistry beaker since college.
Or was it high school?

"Where to begin?" she wondered. Like every other well-trained business student, she knew her way around LinkedIn, the networking site for people seeking internships, investors, or just a foot in the door. On a whim, Sarah typed "cleaning products manufacturer" into the site's search bar. Names came up! She wrote them down. Next, she entered "director of formulation." More names. The talented people she needed actually existed. She was emboldened. She typed "sustainability officer." Several of her searches led to names at Clorox and Procter & Gamble, manufacturers of the cleaning products Sarah wished she could replace. She dropped all the relevant names—around a thousand in total—into an Excel spreadsheet.

One by one, she started emailing the names on her list. She avoided pinging multiple employees at the same company on the same day, worrying they might talk and think she was a wingnut. Her emails were pointed and short—for example, "Can you spare five minutes to share some basics on detergent manufacturing?" How could they say no? Still, it was slow going. Most people didn't even open the emails she sent. When someone did respond, the response was, more often than not, dispiriting. "This can't be done." She heard that a lot. Also: "If soap pills were possible, someone would have made them long ago." Basically, she had forty-some industry veterans tell her, "This is impossible."

She had forty-some industry veterans tell her,
"This is impossible."

At this time, in 2018, the supposed state-of-the-art in-home cleaning products were liquids in tubs (heavy and plastic), loose powders (heavy and often packed in plastic), or pods filled with liquids or loose powders (sneaky polluters packaged in plastic). Sarah wanted to eliminate the big packaging and the pod tech. She sought a complete reinvention of the form.

Back to LinkedIn. This time she searched "chemist" and "chemistry." Within a few clicks, she'd found her four-leaf clover. Syed Naqvi had the perfect credentials. He'd once worked in vitamins—hard-pill manufacturing just like she needed. Now he was director of formulation at Method, only the hottest cleaning brand of the moment. Best of all, he responded immediately. Before blinking, she invented a reason to meet him in San Francisco, where he worked. I'll be out your way next week, she told him. White lie. But he bought it. She jetted out from New York, they met in person, and Sarah—who'd prepared for this meeting over several sleep-less nights—clearly impressed him with her vision. How insane was it, she asked him, that 90 percent of the liquid cleanser regularly filling all our oversized plastic jugs is water? What if we get rid of the water and the throwaway plastic carrier and just sell the concentrated soap? Syed nod-ded. Then, taking his last sip of coffee, he mentioned he was headed to Chicago the next week, for a conference. "Weird. I just happen to have a meeting in the Windy City next week!" she replied. Another white lie. Luckily, their Chicago chat went just as well.

But Sarah had a chicken-and-egg problem. "I couldn't hire him [Syed] to create our product, because I didn't have money. But I couldn't raise money without a product," she explained. She decided to send out a plea through friends and other contacts, making it clear that a star Method for-mulator was keen on her idea and would jump in with both feet if only she had a bit of funding to give him. She quickly raised $3 million. She owed Justin Timberlake a big thank-you note, among others.

Syed joined Sarah's nascent company, but getting going was trickier than he'd expected. He needed a lab, but every space in the Bay Area was too expensive. He thought he might work from home, but manufacturers refused to ship even nontoxic substances like sodium citrate and hydrated silica—basics of cleaning products—to a home address. Sarah finally found an affordable but geographically impossible lab in Missoula, Montana, and laughed when she told Syed about it, sure he'd laugh, too. Instead, he grabbed his cowboy boots and took off for the Big Sky state.

Within a year of joining the company, Syed delivered. Pink, blue, and yellow quarter-sized tablets of bathroom, glass, and multipurpose cleanser. It wasn't easy—he'd tried dozens of iterations. Some of the failed tablets were as big as hockey pucks. Others wouldn't dissolve, or they foamed until they overflowed their receptacles. She knew that the popular "dissolvable" pods were not the right model. They look innocuous enough, but they are anything but. Teenagers were daring each other to eat them (ever heard of the Tide Pod Challenge?) and getting poisoned. But, eventually, he landed on the right formulations. All he and Sarah needed to get their product to market was packaging for her beautiful pills, something to prevent them from breaking apart in high humidity, for example.

Sarah was all over this.

But what would it be made of? She scoured the packaged goods industry. "But all of the machinery that creates packaging has been designed to run on plastic," she said. She was stuck. She was so desperate, she paced the aisles of Whole Foods, looking. "Surely there must be a snack or a candy that is being packaged in compostable packaging?" she thought. There wasn't. Ultimately, she had to invest in a machine to make what she wanted. It cost her hundreds of thousands of dollars to do the right thing.

Even the paint on one of her "starter kits"—containing a reusable acrylic jug and three eucalyptus-mint soap pellets—had to meet strict environmental standards. She blew through three paint manufacturers before finding one that made the grade. Now every kit reads—in safe-for-the-planet paint—"Refill is the new recycle."

"Refill is the new recycle."

In April 2019, Blueland—the name Sarah chose for her company—launched its first products: bathroom, glass, and multipurpose cleaners. That October, she was invited onto *Shark Tank* to pitch her product line. For a tiny company, this was mega exposure, like a $5 million Super Bowl ad, but free. Sarah looked in charge, strutting the stage. This wasn't her first clutch moment, and it showed. In 2011, she'd dropped out of Harvard Business School to help launch a shopping website—a shocking move for the child of Korean immigrants who'd expected their daughter to pick a safe, stable path as a doctor, lawyer, or banker. But the leap had proven to be the right move then, as her current path was now. She didn't break a sweat when judge Mark Cuban hassled her about her agenda. He wasn't convinced she wanted investors so much as free advertising. Cuban was the only doubter, though. She walked away with exactly what she'd asked the judges for—$270,000.

Sarah is pretty sure one particular statistic won her the money. Blueland estimates they can eliminate five billion single-use plastic bottles a year. Even that won't be enough, though. The problem is so much bigger. But one step at a time is our only move, Sarah says. She credits her dad for teaching her this lesson. When she was young, he would ask her, "You know how you eat an elephant?" And she would answer, as he'd taught her, "One bite at a time, Dad."

> **FACT:** Once plastic jugs end up in landfills, they can take up to four hundred years to properly decompose, according to the EPA.

> **FACT:** In 2018, in the US, twenty-six million tons of plastic waste went to landfills. Just three million tons of plastic waste was recycled, according to the EPA.

> **FACT:** In 2019, 180 nations signed on to the Basel Convention agreeing to strict limits on exports of plastic waste from richer countries to poorer ones. One of the few countries that refused to sign: the United States. The US continues a dark history of sending plastic waste to developing nations.

Shampoo Minus the Bottle—Meet Sustainabar

In 2019, Tessa, fourteen, and Davia, eleven, picked up a Lush shampoo bar at the mall. The eco-minded Albany, California, sisters had been wanting to go plastic-free for their hair care. But the bar was a pricey twelve dollars, and afterward their hair was greasy and matted to their heads. So, they tried making their own bars.

Today, the pair is running Sustainabar (www.sustainabar.net) on nights and weekends. Along with shampoo, they are cranking out conditioner, lotion, and dish soap bars (some heart- and leaf-shaped), and shaving cream "pucks." They looked up recipes online and started gathering the tools and ingredients—a digital scale, molds, minerals for shimmer, oils for scent, cocoa and shea butter, coconut oil, and special spatulas. Like all entrepreneurs, they have had their share of mishaps. One time, a batch of soaps was sitting in the oven cooling when Tessa preheated to 375° to get ready to bake cookies. Two dozen just-made melted bars was a bummer, and a mess. Another time, their mom added lye for soap into an aluminum pot, and the pot instantly melted down.

At this point, Sustainabars are selling swiftly online, and they are stocked in three Bay Area retail stores. The sisters are converting people off household plastic one by one. "Our friends, they all use bar shampoo now," Tessa said proudly from her Bay Area home in April 2021.

Jannice Newson

Cofounder

Nana Britwum

Cofounder

Lillian Augusta

Pioneering biodegradable braids

I AM ODDLY GOOD AT: crochet (Jannice) // I can ID any vehicle on the road. I'm oddly obsessed with cars. (Nana)

I AM ODDLY BAD AT: Makeup. Even putting lipstick on evenly is a hassle. // snapping my fingers

THE TRAIT I MOST DEPLORE IN MYSELF: I'm not the most empathetic person. // I'm not tech savvy.

AN OCCASION WHEN I LIE: when people want to hang out and I don't want to // about staying up all night

A WORD OR PHRASE I MOST OVERUSE: "Sponge boy me Bob" (from *SpongeBob*) // "always"

A HABIT I'M TRYING TO GIVE UP: biting my nails // holding on to long-term plans when I should learn to live in the moment

IF I COULD CHANGE ONE HUMAN BEHAVIOR TO SAVE THE PLANET:
greed // Encourage people to think about the life cycle of the products
that they buy. How did it get here? Where is it going?

> **FACT:** Compostable braiding hair extensions are also being made
> using banana fiber extracted from the stem of banana trees.

Braids have always been Nana Britwum's defining look—the only way she
feels like herself. But they have meant an itchy and burning scalp every
day, for most of her life. They've made her wonder, more than once, if she
was doing something very wrong with her hair. . . .

Jannice Newson has fought a similar hair battle. As a girl, she desper-
ately wanted braids but had to settle for relaxer-straightened tresses, a
look that did not marry well with a heavy athletic schedule. "My hair was
sweaty all the time. I looked kind of rough." She finally got braids in college. Easier to manage, but the scalp-burn was unbearable.

These two hair stories collided in 2019 when Jannice and Nana were
assigned the same dorm room at a two-day symposium for young con-
servationists. Chilling on their bunks after the formal events, they probably
should've been talking about the impact of erosion on shrimp populations
in Mississippi, but the topic that had them up half the night was hair. That
is, shared braid misery.

They determined quickly that the culprit was plastic. The synthetic hair
extensions they—and many other Black women—weave in to create styl-
ish cornrows, Bantu knots, and box braids are made out of plastic. Most
synthetic hair is a blend of nylon, polyester, and acrylic, heated and ex-
truded through spinnerets to make hairlike thread. Acrylic has been reported to be a known carcinogen. Now add that most women leave their

braids in for one to three months (because getting them put in takes an entire day and costs around $200), and you've got a recipe for misery. That so many women were walking around wanting to pull out their hair—literally—seemed ridiculous.

That so many women were walking around wanting to pull out their hair—literally—seemed ridiculous.

The bunkmates knew this conversation was just getting started. Lucky for them, they were going home to the same place, the University of Michigan. Jannice was getting her master's degree in natural resources and conservation, and Nana was earning a master's degree in molecular, cellular, and developmental biology. Somehow, they'd never bumped into each other on campus.

Once back in Ann Arbor, they started hanging out. A lot. One day, after another rant session about scalp-burn, Jannice pinged Nana: "We gotta get to it!" It was time to solve this hair thing.

Their scientific experience (they'd each earned a scholarship to study conservation in a special program as undergrads) told them they had to replace the plastic with something organic, probably plant matter. They had seen enough fibrous greenery to recognize that it would have the right consistency. The question was, what specific plant? They researched obvious candidates first—corn and cotton. Neither was quite right.

"What if we used phrag?" Jannice tossed out at the end of a brainstorming session. She was writing her thesis on the sustainability of wetlands. That work had introduced her to a nasty species destroying the Great Lakes coast: phrag. The word is short for "phragmites," an invasive weed that grows stalks up to sixteen feet high and kills native plants by hoarding all the available nutrients. The damage wreaks havoc on fish habitats and property values. "People spend millions trying to get rid of it," Jannice explained.

Using phragmites would solve a boatload of problems. Organic braiding material in abundance. Check. A commercial use for phragmites. Check. Save fragile wetland ecosystems. Check.

And there was a proximity bonus, too: their college town had plenty of the invasive stuff. A few hours after Jannice had her phrag revelation, the two students were driving to Saginaw Forest, ten minutes from Ann Arbor, to harvest some. They chopped down as many armfuls as they could stuff into their car. (Next time they'd bring something better than a kitchen knife.)

By luck, they had ready access to a science lab that had seen its share of plants. Some of their new lab mates made time to teach them how to extract fibers. "We tried a lot of things. We're still trying a lot of things," Nana said. Like whether to use a blend of plants or just phragmites. In 2021, they sent their first working prototype to manufacturers for a small production run. Of course, they will braid the hair on their own heads first, as a test.

No one in the business community had any doubts that the two scholars would find the perfect formula with trial and error. Jannice and Nana have won a head-spinning number of grants, pitch competitions, and awards, including the Essence/McDonald's Making Moves Pitch Competition and the 2020 Michigan Business Challenge. In early 2020, they earned spots in several incubator programs.

Permanent roommates now, Jannice and Nana have a makeshift lab in their home basement, where they can experiment, tinker, and agonize at any time of day or night.

Managing through struggle comes naturally to Nana. Her family moved from Ghana to Lawrence, Kansas, when Nana was four. They were able to immigrate because Nana's mom was a lucky winner in the US visa lottery, and Nana has never lost the sense that she must honor her family's luck by making the most of every opportunity. She whizzed through her AP classes in high school, joined the swim and dive teams, participated in Future Farmers of America, and then went off to Cornell University.

Jannice was a striver from the start, too, the first in her family to attend college, which she did at the University of Missouri. And it only took a field trip to the Chicago Botanic Garden to turn her on to conservation science. She gawked at the garden's docents, talking about wetlands and forests, running their hands through plants, all the employees outside all day. "I was like, 'This is your job?'" She immediately saw a role for herself in that world.

Jannice and Nana never expected to become hair entrepreneurs. But once they started fixating on this hair problem, it wouldn't let them go. "Hair is a super important part of Black culture," Jannice explained. It's been ridiculed, discriminated against, and policed since colonizers first set foot on the African landmass. The texture of Black hair means that braids are sometimes the best way to avoid damage from heat and humidity and to reduce the hassle of caring for it. Some women wear braids to connect with cultural roots, to make a statement, or to signal an unwillingness to cave to pressures to look mainstream. But the plastic in hair extensions complicates things. "Once you start thinking about the plastic on your head, it's hard to stop," Jannice said. They want future generations to wear braids that are compatible with the planet and comfort.

> *"Once you start thinking about the plastic on your head, it's hard to stop."*

If Nana and Jannice solve this puzzle, they will be very well rewarded. That's because hair is big business. Enough women are committed to braids, despite the discomfort, to create a $2.5 billion—and growing—market.

So, what are Nana and Jannice calling their future line of sustainable hair products? Well, Jannice's grandmother Lillian Augusta left Alabama for Chicago during the Great Migration, when six million Black people left the South for a better life in the North. She was a fearless, amazing woman. That is exactly what they wanted their brand to stand for. So, "Lillian Augusta" it is.

Shelby O'Neil

Originator of

No Straw November

The last straw with straws

I AM ODDLY GOOD AT: memorizing areas and maps

I AM ODDLY BAD AT: watching cooking competitions—they stress me out to the max

MY GREATEST FEAR: accidentally driving in a parade (again)

A GUILTY PLEASURE: binge eating Trader Joe's ghost pepper chips and watching Bravo TV shows

THE TRAIT I MOST DEPLORE IN MYSELF: I'm my worst critic over the simplest things.

A TIME I'D RATHER NOT REMEMBER: I got into a bike accident with my mom that resulted in me getting launched off my bike. When I was on the ground, a priest helped me up. I fear seeing him every day.

MY GREATEST ACHIEVEMENT: getting into UC Berkeley and being on *Sesame Street*

SOMETHING I USED TO DO BEFORE I REALIZED HOW BAD IT WAS FOR THE ENVIRONMENT: use face washes with microbeads in them

> **IDEA:** If you use a straw, here are some slick ways to reuse: Cut into sections and slide onto your Kindle, computer, and phone cords to mark the devices as your own. Use as flower holders, to keep a single stem looking pert in a bud vase. Tape one onto the spine of a journal as a pen holder.

It was the boringest of Saturday errands that made Shelby O'Neil an activist. It was 2015, she was fifteen, and her dad had dragged her along to Les Schwab Tires just outside her small central-California farm town of San Juan Bautista (so farm-y that her school mascot was a hay baler). While he discussed tread widths with a salesperson, she hit the waiting room snack table. Mindlessly stuffing her little red-and-white-striped bag with popcorn, she eyed the tray of coffee fixings. Instantly, she was free-falling. . . . "I saw all these tiny stir sticks. Hundreds of them. Straws are wrecking our ocean ecosystems, and no one knew or cared," she recalled. "I was basically having a full-blown breakdown."

By late afternoon, she was madly Googling. She quickly sleuthed out that Farmer Brothers was the nationwide tire chain's coffee supplier. Two more searches and she had the email address for their CEO, Michael Keown.

"Dear Mike," she pecked on her keyboard. "You may not know this, but straws are one of the top ocean polluters. Scientists predict that by 2050, there will be more plastic in the ocean than fish unless we make drastic changes." She told Mike she was a longtime Girl Scout, and in pursuit of her highest-level badge, she had recently founded her own nonprofit, Jr Ocean Guardians. Her group's mission was to grow a youth ocean-protection force, prepped to rid the waters of ecosystem-killing scourges. "I poured my heart out into that email," she recalled.

Two days later, her phone rang. "Hi, Shelby. It's Mike," a deep voice boomed. Turns out, Farmer Brothers CEO Mike Keown was just back from a dive trip in the Maldives, plus had a huge heart for pristine seas. He was floored by her claims. "What!" he exclaimed. "I've never ever thought about this." He complimented her boldness. Then he promised fast changes. Soon his company was delivering bamboo stir sticks instead of straws. "It actually didn't take a lot of persuasion, which is really rare," she said. Future fights would prove harder.

Shelby had every reason to rampage against straws. In the US, five hundred million straws are used every day, according to surveys with straw manufacturers conducted by the Be Straw Free campaign. To picture that number, imagine all those skinny suckers laid end to end. The lineup would wrap the equator two and a half times. (Full disclosure: some conservative-leaning media take issue with this statistic, which has been cited widely in publications from the *New York Times* to *National Geographic*. But even if the right number is half as many, as a pile they'd still weigh as much as one hundred and thirty elephants in a high, blubbery heap.) What makes this ridiculous consumption even worse is that straws are nearly impossible to recycle. They are too lightweight to make it through the mechanical sorter in recycling plants. They fall off the conveyor belt or drop into machine crevices.

"I saw all these tiny stir sticks. Hundreds of them.
Straws are wrecking our ocean ecosystems,
and no one knew or cared," she recalled.

So onward they go to landfills. From there, many escape and migrate into our oceans and rivers, where they break down into smaller and smaller plastic bits, nuggets ingested by fish, and then by birds who eat the fish that ate the plastic—and, well, you get the mess. Seventy-three percent of ocean fish are found to contain microplastics, Shelby stresses, "which means you could be eating a side of plastic with your dinner."

Where did all these straws come from? Legend goes that a man was drinking a mint julep on a summer day in 1880 when the piece of rye grass acting as his straw began to wilt and tear. He tried wrapping strips of paper around a pencil and gluing them together, and by 1890, his factory was mass-producing paper straws.

It was a nasty car accident in middle school that pushed Shelby into ocean evangelism. Her soccer dreams were dashed by a crash that left her with chronic neck pain. Sports became impossible, but not one to sit around, she signed up for every program she could find at the Monterey Bay Aquarium nearby. She ultimately graduated into a Teen Conservation Leader, staffing the main exhibit halls, answering questions from the flood of visitors.

Kids asked the best questions, and the most, which sparked her to launch her nonprofit, Jr Ocean Guardians. She would grow an army of savvy ocean protectors modeled after the beloved Junior Ranger program in America's national parks. She too would have badges that could be earned, and colorful workbooks with spreads on overfishing and floating islands of plastic. For funding, she used every penny of the $6,000 she earned working all summer at the amusement park.

No Straw November was Shelby's breakout idea. She was standing up front in a first-grade classroom, giving her spiel about plastic overrunning the planet. "They were all like 'This is so easy, I'm not going to use any more plastic,'" she said. She loved their gung-ho-ness, but she knew how kids operate. They needed a tangible challenge to keep them honest. So, she threw out a dare: I bet you can't quit straws for the entire month of November. Her challenge went viral. Leonardo DiCaprio put up her blog post about it. Soon she was "straw girl" forevermore. Her feeling was that with an annual practice of thirty straw-free days, people's habits can change. One month of refusing straws, and they would realize how easily they could do without at other times, too. And do without other single use plastic, too.

What Shelby didn't predict was that her straw strike would take flight. The California Coastal Commission pushed a resolution formalizing No Straw November. The Monterey Bay Aquarium took a month off straws, and other aquariums followed. A Girl Scout troop in Okinawa, Japan, joined the fray; the town of Greensboro, North Carolina, passed their own resolution.

Well, thought Shelby, better send some more emails. Her trick is to always write to the CEO directly. One of her notes she pinged into the inbox of Starbucks head Howard Schultz. The CEO of Alaska Airlines received one. Delta Air Lines' leader, too. By now, she has emailed hundreds of CEOs. They are not all receptive. Like the head of one California burger chain who snarled that he felt zero shame about his straws.

But many were responsive. Soon she found herself holding court in a swank, green-accented conference room at Starbucks headquarters in Seattle. She was barely sixteen but already had the good sense to leave her parents in the lobby. "I always tell [young activists] to leave their parents behind. A young person alone makes an impression." She met with the whole Starbucks sustainability team. She shared her models of paper straw options that she'd brought along. They didn't push coffee on her, but they did set up a juice tasting and bring in a pizza.

> *"I always tell [young activists] to leave their parents behind.*
> *A young person alone makes an impression."*

But snacks aside, the meeting left her feeling doubly frustrated. She saw the conflicting pressures on a giant corporation like Starbucks. Even doing away with stir straws is rarely inconsequential and easy. She learned that their see-through plastic cup with its clear dome top is a key element of the brand's marketing plan. How would the Unicorn Frappuccino have become a phenom if tween girls hadn't been able to post on Insta views of the hot-pink drink through a clear top, or protect their whip cloud with magenta sugar dust without that dome, a setup that necessitates a straw? The company also shared plans for their new sippy cup top, which while enabling consumers to go straw-free was just substituting another major hunk of plastic.

At Delta Air Lines, where she was tapped for their first-ever "teen greening" council, ditching plastic was hugely complicated. Touring the headquarters, she observed the involved preflight prep for their in-flight drink service. Straws suddenly seemed like a lone snowflake in a detrimental whiteout. Six-packs of Sprite and club soda were joined with plastic rings (the kind that strangle sea turtles); cases of Coke were shrink-wrapped like mummies in triple-layer plastic wrap. But none of that even mattered once she got wind of the fact that Delta had recently purchased their very own oil refinery. "I felt incredibly defeated. This goes so much deeper than onboard greening. Oh my God, there is so much work to be done," she said.

But none of that even mattered once she got wind of the fact that Delta had recently purchased their very own oil refinery.

Guilting a chain of thirty-nine hospitals off straws came next. Midway through watching *The Simpsons* she caught an ad with a young patient blowing out their birthday candles through a plastic straw. The supposed feel-good spot was promoting Dignity Health. Shelby wrote the CEO, Lloyd Dean, who brought the issue to his sustainability team. Before long, they had cut straw usage in half, to four million annually. Patients still get them—hospitals say patients need them to drink lying down—but visitors do not.

Around this time, Alaska Airlines announced that their twenty-two million plastic stir straws and citrus picks each year would now be made of white birch and bamboo.

In April 2018, Shelby took her cause to the California State Legislature. With her pressure and guidance, State Senator Bill Monning introduced a resolution, cosponsored by Shelby's Jr Ocean Guardians and her long-time workplace, Monterey Bay Aquarium, to formalize No Straw November statewide. Shelby was invited to testify on the resolution before the California Senate Natural Resources Committee. In June, she returned to see Senator Monning bring the resolution to the full Senate, and was horrified standing there beside him in her "fully blinged-out" Girl Scouts vest and sash at how many in the room ultimately voted no. "They wouldn't look me in the eye," she remembered. "Am I really going to cry on the [Senate] floor?" she recalls thinking. This wasn't even a law, just a harmless little resolution. "It was an awakening of how much work remains." But the resolution did get enough ayes to pass, and then moved on to the

State Assembly, where it also got the ayes needed to officially designate the month of November as No Straw November in California. Around the same time, a "Straw upon Request" bill (meaning no straws offered at dine-in restaurants; you have to ask), which Shelby was also active in developing, was introduced and ultimately signed into law by the governor.

She doesn't claim full credit for all the progress. But she is certain that her relentless shaming of CEOs has been productive. Her modest take on her role: "Maybe I was a millisecond of the change."

The environmental reality in her agricultural hometown played a big role in giving her the will and confidence to act. There are so many pesticides in use that their tap water is unsafe for drinking. Someone needs to be speaking up. "If no one else is doing it, then I need to do it," she said.

IV

Fight Club

Varshini Prakash

Cofounder and Executive Director of

the Sunrise Movement

A+ agitator

I AM ODDLY GOOD AT: not taking myself too seriously

I AM ODDLY BAD AT: figuring out new technology

MY GREATEST FEAR: not using my time on earth wisely and fully

THE TRAIT I MOST DEPLORE IN MYSELF: I zone out a lot and people hate it.

AN OCCASION WHEN I LIE: when I sleep through my alarm in the morning

A WORD OR PHRASE I MOST OVERUSE: strategic

A HABIT I'M TRYING TO GIVE UP: eating meals while doing other things

GUILTY PLEASURE: reality tv

FACT: Sunrise Movement youths made a difference in 2020 in electing Green New Deal champions. Collectively, the members sent 2,616,834 texts and 777,570 postcards, and made 5,820,265 calls.

Varshini Prakash has been making a nuisance of herself since she was a wiggly little tot in the 1990s. Her teachers always noted in report cards that she was terribly disruptive.

No surprise, then, that we should find her outside Speaker of the House Nancy Pelosi's office the day after the 2018 midterm elections, demanding attention. She and her fellow protestors—two hundred strong—wore yellow-and-black shirts to match their yellow-and-black banners. "What's your plan?" they shouted at Pelosi. "Do your job! Don't write our death sentence," they screamed.

The caution-tape color scheme was appropriate. Pelosi had a lot to be wary of, because Varshini was formidable. She just got louder and louder and louder that day. "The last major attempt at climate policy was literally in 2009. That was when I was fourteen!" she said, pumping her arm.

"The last major attempt at climate policy was literally in 2009. That was when I was fourteen!"

Then, as if this weren't dramatic enough, in swept Alexandria Ocasio-Cortez, AOC, in her signature heels, ready to kick some serious behind. Reporters and photographers swarmed as intended, spurring more than four thousand news stories.

The Sunrisers—or "Rays Team," as they call themselves—and AOC were demanding that Speaker Pelosi get her House Democrats busy establishing a committee to draft a Green New Deal. Many viewed the demonstration as a turning point in American climate activism. Politico observed that Sunrise has "actually changed the Democratic conversation" around climate, and the *New Yorker* called Sunrise a "dominant influence on the environmental policy of the Democratic Party's young, progressive wing." And AOC, who they had wooed into their corner, was the spark plug that supercharged this moment—Sunrise's secret weapon.

Less than three months later, on February 7, 2019, AOC formally introduced the manifesto in both the House and the Senate, demanding jobs, justice, equity, and environmental urgency that Varshini and her growing green army had been urging: the Green New Deal. This would be "a new national, social, industrial and economic mobilization on a scale not seen since World War II and the New Deal era," the text read. We would meet "100 percent of the power demand in the United States through clean, renewable, and zero-emission energy sources" within a decade. And Varshini was the new face of that impatience.

Varshini was destined for her role. First, she was actually born on Earth Day, in 1994 in Acton, Massachusetts. At age eleven, she watched CNN in horror as a tsunami destroyed her grandmother's home city of Chennai, India. The image of the ocean dragging away trees, homes, and bodies lodged deep in her cranium. The news said "climate change" was to blame. The message stuck. But, Varshini wondered, how could we humans beat an angry Mother Nature? She collected canned foods and brought them to the Red Cross, but it didn't feel like nearly enough.

How could we humans beat an angry Mother Nature?

At the University of Massachusetts, Amherst, she found a better answer. It was 2013 and she'd wandered into an organizing meeting to fight the university's investments in the fossil fuel industry. Many rich colleges put their money into oil and gas stocks, which further lines the pockets of those polluting industries. Students wanted an end to these investments—a process known as "divestment." Varshini listened. She showed up at the next meeting, and the one after that.

Soon she found herself at her first real demonstration, a mass gathering in Washington, DC, to protest the Keystone XL pipeline, which would run from Alberta, Canada, to Steele City, Nebraska, through the critical Ogallala Aquifer, which provides water to the Midwest. Varshini said that standing in a sea of forty thousand, listening to indigenous elders calling for protection of their land and water, "just lit a fire under me." Back on campus, she doubled her commitment to green activism, starting with circulating petitions and hanging banners; almost all were about the fossil fuel industry's death grip on the environment.

Then, on a frigid December day during finals week, she moved to center stage. At a protest fighting a new fracking project in the nearby Pioneer Valley, an organizer thrust the megaphone into her hand. Varshini had not intended to speak. "You got this," the mentor encouraged. And Varshini did. The words came easily. She was a natural.

But the megaphone was not enough that time. Future meetings with administrators about the fracking went nowhere. "We got laughed out of the room," Varshini said.

They had to do more, they had to stop the college's habit of business as usual. Varshini came to see disruption as a critical approach. Shortly after, she organized a weeklong takeover of the administration building, with hundreds of students occupying the hallways in shifts starting at six a.m. "I think there was a sense [of] 'These kids aren't going to go away,'"

Varshini reflected. The school's leadership was suddenly listening. Just after Varshini graduated, University of Massachusetts became the first major university to end all oil and gas investments. The victory was sweet.

After graduation, she continued her protest work. A small group of engaged peers started communicating regularly. Some had pushed divestment on their own campuses; others came from movements like Occupy Wall Street (fighting corporate greed and income disparity). Casual text strings among these new, like-minded friends gave way to conference calls and meetups. The group convened wherever it could find free sofas to crash on—a community center here, an uncle's farm there.

That whole first year they dedicated to educating themselves on social change. This began with studying successful large-scale movements. They dug deep into the tactics of the Wide Awakes (abolitionists of the 1800s), the civil rights movement, the fight for gay marriage, women's suffrage, liberation of India under Gandhi. They were thinking big.

The group latched on to the 1955–1956 Montgomery, Alabama, bus boycott as a model. Rosa Parks's refusal to vacate her seat that day did not just spontaneously set off masses of citizens refusing to ride the buses, and trigger the rollback of segregation. Civil rights leaders had been looking for ways to challenge the treatment of African Americans in Montgomery for some time. So after her arrest, they worked quickly and deliberately to leverage the incident to instigate a mass action. Those activists recognized that Parks, highly respected in her community, would make a sympathetic plaintiff for a lawsuit challenging the segregation ordinance, so they pushed her to file. Her court hearing date was targeted as ideal for producing momentum to launch the boycott, so activists printed and distributed stacks of flyers advertising that date and calling for avoiding the bus. On the day before, a Sunday, local ministers were coached to spread the word to their congregations. The result was that 90 percent of Blacks in Montgomery stayed off the buses on December 5, 1955. Ultimately, in 1956, the US Supreme Court struck down laws requiring segregated seating on public buses.

As Varshini explained, "The role of a movement is being able to shift public opinion." She too would create similarly dramatic actions, designed to maximize press coverage and public outrage.

Now their movement-in-the-making needed a name. These were dark days for the planet. President Trump, an anti-science climate change denier, had just moved into the White House. Slashing environmental protections was his favorite hobby besides tweeting. Still, Varshini and her crew believed they would bring the change, "as sure as the sun would rise." They were the Sunrise Movement.

The group floated their new organizational name and edict at the 2017 People's Climate March in Washington, DC. They canvassed the crowd, asking for feedback. Just as important, they gathered signatures of people who wanted to join them. By day's end, Sunrise had its first thousand members. Building a list is the foundation of movement organizing.

Next, they held an activist training in Philadelphia. Twenty-five attendees showed. They reviewed the book *Rules for Revolutionaries: How Big Organizing Can Change Everything* and the basics of messaging. Varshini and her fellow leaders hammered the message of consistency and clarity. To save the planet, they needed to articulate

the problem and the solution in one succinct story. By Sunday, Varshini and team had made a direct request of the new recruits: go back home and start a Sunrise chapter.

By the midterm elections of 2018, Sunrise had fifteen "hubs." Electing progressive, climate-advocate candidates became the group's driving mission. They did mass youth voter registration and turnout efforts. They focused on key races like Michigan and Pennsylvania. Devotion to the cause often meant living and working together in Sunrise "movement houses" for twenty-four-hour-a-day political pressure.

Within six months, there were Sunrise hubs from Kodiak, Alaska, to Clearwater, Florida—more than four hundred. Today these hubs span the globe.

Varshini plans Sunrise actions like theater productions. These are not slapdash affairs. The occupation of Pelosi's office was plotted like a high-stakes diamond heist. The group cased the area outside her office the day before to identify points of maximum visual impact. Photography is always top of mind. The advance team figures out where to shoot photos, and from what angle. They have mapped out where people will stand, how they will stand, what their signs will say—like stage directors. They produce color-coordinated signage in a uniform font. Everything is geared toward creating shareable, high-impact photos that will reach far beyond the in-person protests. In other words, going viral.

The occupation of Pelosi's office was plotted like a high-stakes diamond heist.

Yet, sometimes even the most painstaking planning flops. As the 2020 election neared, Varshini's Philadelphia team planned a sit-in at local Democratic Party offices to demand a stronger environmental platform. As often happens at Sunrise demonstrations, police came, and protesters were arrested for illegal occupation. The problem on this day was that the Sunrisers were not at Democratic Party offices. They had the wrong address. Nevertheless, they got press, maybe even more so for the snafu.

But plenty of demonstrations go off flawlessly. To pressure the Democratic National Committee to devote a presidential debate to climate, they slept on the steps of the committee's DC offices. They failed to get a full debate but convinced CNN to do a climate town hall (and received midnight pizza on the steps, courtesy of Bernie Sanders's staff).

Arguably, groups like Sunrise are the reason why more than 70 percent of Americans believe in climate change and want it resolved.

Today the fidgety girl born on Earth Day whose mom sent her to school in traditional Indian garb, who always felt like an outsider, is finding herself on the inside. During the Democratic primaries, her group rated Joe Biden an F for his climate platform. Now she is serving on his presidential climate task force. One positive of having clout: she applied pressure that helped move his timeline to decarbonize the power sector from 2050 to 2035. Sunrise, sunrise, sunrise.

Change Minds: Write a Persuasive Op-Ed

Put down your protest sign and hit your keyboard. A thought-provoking opinion piece published in a newspaper or online editorial page can make real ripples, especially now, with social media's magnifying power. The voices of young people are in hot demand as they are leading today's environmental movement. Shifting culture and policy starts with getting ideas accepted by the mainstream, and opinion pieces are key to doing that. Instilling hope and providing action items is more effective than doomsday speak. Humor is a rarity in this space, which is why when it's used effectively, it can be a potent tactic. According to OpEd Project, approximately 80 percent of published op-eds are by guys, so there is a major push to elevate women's voices. Try these tips to write an op-ed that provokes action:

1. Hook readers by starting with a surprising fact. If fast fashion is your burning issue, an attention-grabbing opener might be this personal revelation: "Feeling virtuous driving my load of give-away clothes to Goodwill, I had no clue that over 80 percent of discarded items get burned or buried in a landfill."
2. Tie your piece to current news. The day after a wildfire breaks out nearby is the moment to offer up your view that Smokey the Bear may be cute, but he has led us astray. His message to put out every fire is dead wrong. An unexpected take gets noticed, read, and shared. We would imagine that extinguishing every flame is ideal, but actually dead wood buildup from not letting fires burn naturally is exacerbating the frequency and size of forest fires.

3. Get to the point. Come out swinging rather than making the reader hang in for a few paragraphs to get your point. The whole piece should typically be around five hundred to eight hundred words and have a strong point and point of view.

4. Use the OpEd Project (www.theopedproject.org) as a resource. The site lists many publications where you can pitch opinion pieces, and provides contact info and submission guidelines. The site provides advice for strengthening your argument. They also offer opinion-piece writing workshops—with scholarships available to cover the cost.

5. Tell a story that only you can tell. Maybe your family raised cattle and then you all became vegetarians, or you convinced your high school to install wind power (a teen did this in Massachusetts).

Annie Leonard

Executive Director of

Greenpeace USA

and Creator of

The Story of Stuff

Global waste-tracker

I AM ODDLY GOOD AT: Sharing. My friends and I share clothes, cars, tools, baking supplies, a "birthday box" of decorations.

I AM ODDLY BAD AT: stepping aside and ensuring others have space to share their perspectives, too

THE TRAIT I MOST DEPLORE IN MYSELF: When I am excited, I don't listen well.

AN OCCASION WHEN I LIE: When someone asks me to do something, and I feel too guilty to say no, I say, "Sure, I'd be happy to do that" when I really won't be happy doing that.

A WORD OR PHRASE I MOST OVERUSE: "awesome." But in my defense, there is so much in the world that is awesome! Go for a hike if you don't believe me!

A HABIT I'M TRYING TO GIVE UP: working so many hours that I don't get enough exercise

SOMETHING I USED TO DO BEFORE I REALIZED HOW BAD IT WAS FOR THE ENVIRONMENT: Eat meat. Especially octopus—my goodness, they are so intelligent. We really need to stop eating them.

> **IDEA:** University of New Hampshire pioneered an end-of-year move-out program called Trash 2 Treasure to deal with the mountains of waste students leave behind each year. In 2013, Eckerd College in Saint Petersburg, Florida, adopted the program, and by 2019 had diverted 58 tons of books, beer cozies, clothes, furniture, and junk from landfill. Each year, the program is run by six or so student interns who are paid using proceeds from sales of some of the items.

Every morning of her freshman year, Annie Leonard walked the six blocks from 110th Street up to 116th to Barnard College. A world apart from her serene, moist, green Pacific Northwest, New York City was a circus for her senses—Carts of steaming hot dogs! Bright yellow taxis! Shrieking sirens! Going uptown, the sidewalks were remarkably clean, the magic of late-night street sweepers. But coming home, the world around her looked trashed. Literally. Piles upon piles of black plastic bags, the mounds mostly higher than her head. It seemed like each apartment dweller must have been dumping all their possessions every single day.

What could possibly be filling all those bags?

Well, one day, her curiosity won out. She tore into a green Hefty bag topping a heap on 113th Street. Out spilled pizza boxes, Snickers wrappers, grocery receipts, junk mail, an old bio textbook, newspapers, flyers. Holy mountain of paper! A half block down, she ripped into another. Paper bonanza again. She was shocked.

A memory flooded her brain: She was a high school junior working in the northern Cascades with the Youth Conservation Corps. She had been hiking along, when she suddenly stopped, dumbstruck, seeing her first mass expanse of clear-cut trees, "shaved clean like the head of a prison inmate," she recalled. Thousands of trees felled for paper mills. It was an alarming sight then. Now, on 113th Street, she felt downright sick. "I thought, 'Really, you are destroying my beloved forest to fill these bags with pizza boxes and corporate flyers?'"

"I thought, 'Really, you are destroying my beloved forest to fill these bags with pizza boxes and corporate flyers?'"

That was 1982. Annie fell into garbage that day and has never climbed out. Her next semester at Barnard, as part of an environmental studies class, she visited Fresh Kills Landfill on Staten Island. This was where those bags she'd seen ended up. It was an ocean of waste clear to the horizon. In every direction. So much of it looked perfectly usable, too—a television, dictionaries, a baby doll in a lacy dress, a leather handbag, a can opener. . . . Why did people throw away perfectly good stuff? Didn't someone else want it?

The Fresh Kills Landfill, when closed in 2002, was the largest trash heap on the planet, with ten tons of stuff arriving annually while it had been operating.

The sheer quantity of garbage from one city stressed Annie out. She'd been raised by a single mom, a school nurse, in a family that scrimped and saved and barely had enough. They produced little trash because they had few things to throw away. What they had, they repaired. Shoes got resoled, backpack zippers replaced.

After college, Annie went to work for Greenpeace. The advocacy organization was investigating some instances of illegal toxic waste dumping. One day, her boss asked, "Who here wants to go follow the waste, find out where it's being sent?" Annie couldn't get her hand up fast enough.

She became a professional waste-tracker. For eight years, she crisscrossed the globe—Bangladesh, South Africa, China, India. She trained as a private investigator, learning how to get the information no one wants you to get. She carried a fake ID. She snuck into factories, posing as a bike messenger. She spied on what was being made, what was left over, and where the discards went. Companies in the US had filled up so many domestic dumps that they had started shipping waste overseas, to poor places with fewer detection systems to root out wrongdoing.

A smelting plant in South Carolina was secretly mixing hazardous ash—emptied from the filters topping smokestacks—into fertilizer and selling it to Bangladeshi farmers. Off she went to Bangladesh with her Lonely Planet guidebook, where she set up camp in a youth hostel and headed out daily to collect soil samples. "I'd leave a note in the room, 'If I don't come back . . . I went to "X" place to track where this shipment went.'" In a Black township in South Africa, a British company was dumping mercury into the river. Her tests revealed levels eight thousand times above normal.

"I'd leave a note in the room, 'If I don't come back . . . I went to "X" place to track where this shipment went.'"

When she returned to the US, she had visited hundreds and hundreds of manufacturing facilities and dumps and ship loading docks. She had seen the sinister ways that certain companies and even countries operated, things that once you see, you never forget. She wasn't sure what to do next, where to take her information. While she was regrouping, she got invited to participate in a yearlong leadership training program. The group was a who's who of the social activism world. They ended up meeting quarterly, and one piece of the agenda was to speak for five minutes on your life's purpose. "I thought, 'This is awesome. This is my chance to get all these people to care about garbage,'" she said.

Her turn came, and she launched right in. "We make too many materials," she began. The group looked lost before she even uttered her second sentence. The feedback was harsh. "I have no idea what you just said. I don't even know what a material is," someone told her. After two more flops, she had one final chance.

This time, she pretended she was talking to kids. She drew planet Earth on the whiteboard. Pointing to it, she said, "This is where we start." She added a square that she labeled "factory," a small house, and a box that she labeled "dump." She then drew arrows indicating the one-way movement of stuff, starting with resources extracted from the earth, which go to factories to become stuff, and then go to homes for use, and, in almost no time, go to the dump. "This is the story of stuff." She went on explaining how we chop down the trees, blow up the mountains to get the metals, use up all the water. "We are cutting and mining and hauling and trashing the place so fast that we are undermining the planet's very ability for people to live here." She paused for emphasis. "Did you know that 99 percent of the stuff we harvest, mine, process, and transport is trashed within six months of purchase? How did we get so far away from stewardship and thrift?" When she finally stopped and took a breath, the room erupted in applause.

She had found her story. The story of stuff was what she knew. The story of stuff was what she needed to sound the alarm on. She started giving this talk to small groups. A funder in one group was so excited that he said he'd pay her to make this into a film. This was 2006. She considered it. She'd given her spiel over a hundred times. She could give it a hundred more times or make a film and possibly reach thousands or even more ears. Eventually her film, *The Story of Stuff,* debuted. Seven million people in two hundred countries would see it. In twenty short minutes on-screen, she explained overconsumption and the problem of our "more is better" capitalist system. She got hundreds of thousands of emails asking her "What can I do to help?"

Short films get through to people. So, she kept making them—and made fourteen in all. *The Story of Bottled Water. The Story of Cap & Trade.* Electronics. Cosmetics. Change. *The Story of Solutions* . . . She helped launch a whole educational organization called the Story of Stuff.

That was fun and impactful and all, but in 2014 she decided she had to get far more political, to find a perch where she could speak out, drive a movement, pressure politicians to make the kind of policy changes that could actually save our proverbial bacon. So she went back to her starting place—Greenpeace USA. Today she runs the whole darned organization. Its central mandate is to sound the alarm on global environmental problems, using attention-getting campaigns and peaceful protests to promote solutions.

Greenpeace got its start with an act of civil disobedience, which means acting out publicly—sometimes breaking the law, but peacefully—to achieve visibility for a cause. The very first act was to protest nuclear testing. A small group of activists leased a fishing vessel and set sail for Amchitka Island in Alaska. That was where some nuclear testing was occurring, and the idea was to place themselves in harm's way as a form of protest. The activists were intercepted by the Coast Guard, but still succeeded in bringing worldwide attention to the danger of nuclear testing. Since then, Greenpeace USA has used activism to fight commercial whaling, protect Antarctica, protest fossil fuels, fight Coca-Cola's and PepsiCo's reign of single-use plastics, and so much more.

Annie walks her talk, too. She keeps her carbon footprint low by living in a modern commune with six old friends—in a row of connected houses. They share gardens. They babysit one another's kids. They exchange tools. "When I need an egg, I don't get in my car and use gas. I walk next door," she says.

> **ACTION:** Go visit your local dump. And when you travel, check out a dump in the new place. Once you see our trash problem, you cannot unsee it.

Check It Out!
Boost Your Sharing Game at the Library.

In the ever more digital world, libraries are a bit of a relic. But don't toss that library card. You will be shocked at all you can borrow instead of buy. Need a Santa suit? At the Bolivar County Library in Mississippi, they rent those out. Prom dresses cost a bundle and rarely get a second wearing. Talk about a landfill bomb. Well, the Dallas Public Library and the Elmwood Park Public Library in Illinois both have gowns to loan. In Brooklyn, New York, you can get your music ya-yas out by checking out a keyboard or electric guitar from the central branch of the Brooklyn Public Library. If you'd rather play games than instruments, board games can be borrowed there, too. In wintry Telluride, Colorado, the local library checks out snowshoes, but also Kindles, sewing machines, and even a karaoke machine.

If you are inspired by these ideas but your library isn't on board yet, talk to the librarian about starting an innovative lending program. Or, better yet, offer to lead the effort.

Sharing is cool. There is no reason we all need to own tools, odd kitchen appliances, gear for seldom-done sports, and so much more. Start swapping instead of buying.

Rhiana Gunn-Wright

Director of

Climate Policy at the Roosevelt Institute

and Architect of

the Green New Deal

Nothing short of an eco-mastermind

I AM ODDLY GOOD AT: picking snacks

I AM ODDLY BAD AT: spatial reasoning

MY GREATEST FEAR: causing other people trauma

THE TRAIT I MOST DEPLORE IN MYSELF: how hard it can be for me to trust myself, especially when people I love disagree with me

AN OCCASION WHEN I LIE: when my mom asks me if I remembered to send a thank-you note

A WORD OR PHRASE I MOST OVERUSE: "truly"

A HABIT I'M TRYING TO GIVE UP: forgetting to wash my face at night

IF I COULD CHANGE ONE HUMAN BEHAVIOR TO SAVE THE PLANET, IT WOULD BE: dismissing people we see as less powerful or intelligent

Before Rhiana Gunn-Wright was an eco-mastermind, she was a twenty-three-year-old fangirl working in the White House. Every morning in the summer of 2011, she proudly flashed her ID and marched into the East Wing to make her way to the little desk in the hallway outside First Lady Michelle Obama's office.

Michelle Obama!

Rhiana, a Black woman from the South Side of Chicago, could not believe her proximity to another Black woman from the South Side of Chicago, aka, the First Lady. The job post was a total rush. Rhiana was so close to a role model, so close to the most powerful people in the world. Her whole life, she'd wondered who made the decisions that affected her life. And here she was seeing those people close up, at least from one angle. The First Lady had almost no funding or formal authority, but it didn't seem to matter—Michelle influenced policy. She pushed girls' education around the world and got kids moving in America. "It taught me there are different currencies in the world," Rhiana said—a lesson she would not soon forget.

Sadly, cozy girlfriend chats with Michelle never materialized; Rhiana's only meeting with her was during the obligatory end-of-year formal photograph, a perk for staffers. "Ohhh, you're the girl behind the desk," the First Lady said, flashing Rhiana her famous big grin. "Great, I'm the girl behind the desk," Rhiana thought. "Well, at least Michelle recognizes me."

Today Rhiana would definitely get more than an obligatory hello from the most powerful people in the White House.

That's because, in 2019, she was suddenly thrust into the spotlight. Everyone—CNN, the *New York Times,* MSNBC, *Pod Save America,* Bloomberg, Vox, *Essence, Marie Claire,* National Public Radio—credited Rhiana as the "architect" behind the Green New Deal, the sweeping environmental and social agenda for America proposed by the progressive wing of the Democratic Party.

Receiving this credit was a mixed bag. She was certainly not the sole creator, by any stretch. The work and thinking had been a team effort. And the term "Green New Deal" for a grand plan to transform the economy and society to meet the challenges of climate change had been floating around in liberal circles for years. Plus, the Green New Deal was and still is controversial. Republicans find it hair-raising, expensive, pie-in-the-sky. Progressives call it barrier-smashing, essential, the only plan that could save us all. Both sides agree on one thing: it is bold. As bold, some argue, as Franklin D. Roosevelt's New Deal, unveiled more than eighty years ago. Back then, America was facing the Great Depression, a dire time of bread lines, mass unemployment, drought, and economic free fall. To dig us out quickly, Roosevelt launched a fleet of government projects—new highways, bridges, airports, youth work programs—to jump-start the economy. It worked. The Green New Deal (GND) of 2019 springs from a similar moment of national urgency, or more correctly, worldwide urgency. It calls for the launch of an all-hands-on-deck mobilization to get to net-zero carbon emissions by 2050, led by the United States, which has historically been responsible for a disproportionate quantity of greenhouse emissions. The reference to the original New Deal was, of course, intended.

Both sides agree on one thing: it is bold.
As bold, some argue, as Franklin D. Roosevelt's New Deal.

Environmentalists have been clamoring for these kinds of formal plans for decades. What's novel and astonishing about the Green New Deal—what's earned Rhiana such plaudits—is that it proposes to fix the environment and our most pressing societal problems at the same time.

The Green New Deal reimagines America on two levels: first, the societal level, tackling racism, income inequality, jobs, healthcare, childcare, and housing; second, the environmental level, overhauling the electricity grid, changing infrastructure, building renewables, upgrading buildings for energy efficiency, etc. The breakthrough of it is seeing the complete interconnectedness of the issues. It means it's a no-go to ship trash from the suburbs to an inner-city incinerator, where poor inhabitants then suffer from air pollution. Also a no-go: disregarding Indigenous communities' treaties in order to build an oil pipeline.

One could argue that Rhiana's childhood provided the blueprint for the Green New Deal. She was raised by a single mom, poor, in a neighborhood too close to dump sites and factories. African Americans are 75 percent more likely than other Americans to live in areas situated near facilities that produce hazardous waste, an NAACP and Clean Air Task Force report found.

The air on the South Side of Chicago probably gave Rhiana asthma, which is a common affliction among kids in low-income areas. Then her mom got sick when Rhiana was eleven. Mysterious blisters began appearing on her skin, which got worse and worse. By the time someone diagnosed the autoimmune condition, two years later, her mom was close to death, and Rhiana had PTSD from nearly losing her. Her public high school was so poorly funded, her mom sent her hours away to a free public boarding school. There she faced discrimination, people who "didn't take kindly to a smart Black girl."

Her academic gifts, though, catapulted her into a new world. She attended Yale. She got her master's degree in social policy at Oxford on a Rhodes Scholarship. Always, her work pointed her back toward home, to the issues of her community. She volunteered at a center for pregnant teens. In her job at the Institute for Women's Policy Research, she lobbied for a federal paid maternity leave benefit. She headed up policy for Michigan gubernatorial candidate Abdul El-Sayed, who pledged to achieve 100 percent renewable energy; he had been her boss at the Detroit Health Department, which was where health and the environment first collided in her brain. Up until then, her focus had been on poverty, writing policy papers to help the woman standing in line for public childcare assistance. What did solar panels have to do with that woman in line? And then it clicked.

Always, her work pointed her back toward home, to the issues of her community.

In 2018, Rhiana became policy director at a think tank, New Consensus. A think tank is basically a research lab that churns out ideas to improve society. New Consensus was "putting the meat on the bones," as Rhiana said, of a vision for a more equitable and environmental society. As head of policy, by January 2019, she had distilled all these ideas into a tight social science paper, which she published in collaboration with a Cornell University law professor. The paper, "The Green New Deal: Mobilizing for a Just, Prosperous, and Sustainable Economy," was a framework for a new societal vision, with creating jobs, addressing climate change, and achieving social justice as the guiding lights.

Congresswoman Alexandria Ocasio-Cortez was keenly interested in this vision. She was determined to put climate front and center in the national conversation, and she was looking for the language and framework to articulate her overarching vision. She found that, ready to go, in black and white in the work of Rhiana and her New Consensus colleagues, and all their collaborators who helped. So in February 2019, AOC introduced in Congress a formal resolution—a fancy term for a set of ideas being floated for approval but carrying no legal weight and prompting no specific legislative action—based on essentially the very same Green New Deal concept.

Soon after, AOC and her cosponsor, Senator Ed Markey, formally asked Congress to vote on the GND as a nonbinding resolution. Rhiana watched as the Senate's Republican majority voted the resolution down—mocking the plan as "a socialist takeover" and a "ride around on a high-speed light rail" powered by "unicorn tears." It will take away cheeseburgers, Senator Tom Cotton quipped. (Cow farts do mean methane, and methane does hurt the environment. . . .) Even many Democrats were skeptical, viewing the massive scope as unrealistic. Nancy Pelosi referred to it as the "green new dream."

Rhiana had thought she'd have more time to perfect this policy work before it would see the light of day. She wishes she could've gotten more specific, especially around the issue of cost. The estimated cost to implement the Green New Deal ranges from $10 trillion to $93 trillion. That's a big disparity. More detail in the plan would have led to a more accurate estimate.

Still, she is proud of the Green New Deal; whatever it costs is what we must spend, she says. She continues to insist on action, now from a new perch directing climate policy at the Roosevelt Institute, a wonky think tank conceiving how the world ought to work, known for convincing decision-makers to actually make their ideas happen to help people. "This is a crisis. It's here. Climate change isn't going to stop. If proposed solutions are not of the magnitude to bring down emissions, it doesn't matter that they are bipartisan and cheap." Her point is that if an asteroid were hurtling toward Earth and someone came up with an expensive way to stop it, we wouldn't just say, "Nope, too pricey. Let 'er rip." We'd do something, fast.

If an asteroid were hurtling toward Earth and someone came up with an expensive way to stop it, we wouldn't just say, "Nope, too pricey. Let 'er rip." We'd do something, fast.

Rhiana is also certain that equity, environmental justice, and saving the planet go hand in hand. We need to be deliberate about addressing these problems. "If you say no one is expendable, no person is expendable, no community is expendable, that changes how you solve problems," says Rhiana. "Equity doesn't happen on accident. You don't bump into it. You create it."

As polarizing and unfinished as the Green New Deal is, it's still turning heads. For the very first time, every 2020 Democratic presidential candidate put forward a climate campaign agenda; the environment was a topic no one could get around. When Joe Biden got the job, he assembled a climate "nerve center" within his first week, the largest team of climate change experts ever assembled in the White House. The Green New Deal and Rhiana put the issue on the map, forever.

> **FACT:** Approximately 13 percent of African American children have asthma, compared to 7 percent of white children. The death rate for African American children with asthma is one per 1 million, while for white children it is one per 10 million, according to an NAACP report.

Marina DeBris

Trash Artist

Creating "trashion" to
make us all think before we buy

I AM ODDLY GOOD AT: housecleaning

I AM ODDLY BAD AT: drawing

MY GREATEST FEAR: getting lost at night, running out of gas

A GUILTY PLEASURE: Coffee, wine, chocolate. I'm not giving them up. They are all organic and fair trade.

THE TRAIT I MOST DEPLORE IN MYSELF: negativity

AN OCCASION WHEN I LIE: When I'm laying out my rubbish on the sand to write "Help" or "SOS," if authorities give me a hard time, I'll come up with some sort of evasion, like 'Oh, I'm just cleaning up . . .'"

A WORD OR PHRASE I MOST OVERUSE: "like"

A HABIT I'M TRYING TO GIVE UP: staying in my comfort zone

Every morning, Marina DeBris combs Coogee Beach or the sand strip along tiny Gordons Bay for art materials. While both sites are in Sydney, Australia, Gordons Bay is usually a better bet because a storm drain washes right onto the beach, sweeping trash from the street across the sand. Jackpot. A good day is one with a lot of washed-up crap.

A haul in March 2021 resulted in: five light-blue disposable face masks, three pairs of swim goggles (one pink, two green), one and a half to-go coffee cup tops, one Invisalign aligner (not the first she's found), a ribbed tank top, a plastic robot, a tennis ball, a lemon, a bit of red string, a purple bucket, two baggie ties, a sun visor with a plastic brim, the sprayer part of a spray bottle, a tangle of fishing line, a mini soy sauce bottle (empty), and a shred of a pink balloon. Assessment: a pretty typical day. No dentures. No mannequin's leg. No nineteen Santa hats (collected on December 26 a few years before).

Marina, originally from Australia but living for a stint in the US, returned to the "Land Down Under" from Los Angeles in 2015 after California priced her out. At first she was picking up every piece of trash she passed in her new home. But she is not a beach cleaner; she's an artist. Her medium is beach trash. What compels her is the humdrum everyday stuff like Band-Aids, baggie ties, plastic forks, straws, and plastic bottles. She's drawn to the materials that make us think about the decisions we make on a day-to-day basis. Like walking into the ocean wearing a Band-Aid, which will surely float off.

She's drawn to the materials that make us think about the decisions we make on a day-to-day basis.

When Marina feels particularly outraged by the day's mess, she will let out her feelings right there on the beach. She kneels down, dumps her bag like you might your Halloween candy, and arranges everything into giant letters spelling "SOS" or into a big frowny face. At the end of the day, no matter what she's found, she dresses up the squat metal poles at the beach entrance like they're mannequins—for example, a discarded bikini top, a bucket for a hat, swim goggles, and a mask.

People like to gather around to see what she's doing. Good. Often, they call her names, tell her she's a loser. Bad. Once a government official in his little vehicle chased her up the street. Very bad. "It was scary." Still, nobody stops Marina DeBris (not the name she was born with, in case you were wondering, but that's what she's called herself since 2009).

She's had this quiet rebellious streak for a while. At age eleven, living in the Connecticut suburbs, she stopped brushing her hair and grew dreadlocks. She knew her mom, a photographer, would hate her look, which was the idea. She was sick of being a model in her mom's pictures, which often landed in textbooks that they used at school. "I would be the stock photo for a science book chapter on disorders like OCD. I'd be the girl washing the window incessantly. It was mortifying," she said. Still, her mom was Marina's gateway to fine art. More accurately, Marina was constantly dragged into New York City, to museums and galleries. She didn't love it then, but the trips made an impression. She started dabbling in art at home. Sometimes, she and her mom worked together, making embellishments for clothes and bags.

Marina's first foray into her own art was metalsmithing. She did a jewelry-making program in high school and fell for the craft. She went to Indiana University to a special metalsmithing program. But shortly after arriving, she started questioning the practicality of making a living this way. She switched to graphic design. This inspired a transfer to the Rhode Island School of Design, where she finished her degree. These were the days before computer-aided graphic design, when you cut out every letter and laid out pages by hand. She loved working with her hands.

After a few years in the business, however, she felt her soul dying. She was little more than an advertiser, and she was working for big corporations whose practices she hated. "That is who had the money for the kind of campaigns I did," she said. The field was also going more and more digital. Her hands were doing everything on computers.

At this time, in 2009, she was living on Venice Beach, in Los Angeles. She was a runner then, and she would jog the beach and feel ill about the trash she started noticing everywhere. "Have I been asleep for thirty or forty years of my life?" she said, wondering how she was only now noticing the litter explosion. At first, she would gather tall stacks of Styrofoam cups and foil chips packages and walk them up the street to the 7-Eleven to "return them" and make a point. "But I soon realized that this wasn't really attacking the root problem."

She decided to make art to express her distress. The emotions that she hopes to evoke are the ones she feels: "Horror and disgust." "All my work is looking at our species from above and going 'What the hell?'" She hopes to force people to not look away any longer.

> *The emotions that she hopes to evoke are the ones she feels: "Horror and disgust."*

Her first big sensation was "trashion"—fashion made from sorted trash, such as a long skirt made entirely of found balls, from Super Balls to basketballs, and all sizes in between. A white strapless party dress made entirely of Styrofoam to-go containers—cups and bowls make the top, and then the skirt of trays and plates poofs exaggeratedly out at the waist. A bustier of colorful straws, with plastic forks hanging down all around.

A free-form frock made entirely of caution tape. The culminating exhibit for some of her best pieces was a fashion show in 2011 at the swank LA retailer Fred Segal in celebration of Ocean Awareness Week.

Her clothing is meant to be arresting, not beautiful. She never washes any of her found trash, so the smell of seaweed and rot are part of the experience. A floor-length gown of plastic bags is filthy, tinted slightly brown with dirt. If there's half a dead crab hanging off, all the better. Unlike some of the other "girls who green the world," who are all about repurposing castaways into desirable goods, she definitely does not want to be part of today's trend of making hip upcycled outfits, fashions that make junk look really beautiful. "I want to show the true ugliness of these things. Not nifty ways to reuse."

Her clothing is meant to be arresting, not beautiful.
If there's half a dead crab hanging off, all the better.

An installation she calls *Inconvenience Store* really hammered her point home. This idea began as a paper catalogue art piece, listing all the items you would find in one of your favorite lifestyle-brand catalogues. Only, everything was photos of her found trash. This evolved into a fully realized store, packed with items, each individually packaged, cleverly labeled and artfully displayed. She had a builder create a structure. Inside, a junked wire sunglass rack she found on the street holds a dozen pairs of trashed sunglasses, some with broken frames or no lenses. Under the counter is a display of gum, each pack labeled "Gummed Up," and below those, a row of neat little packets of Band-Aids—"Bad aids." There are "Beached Towels," socks, underwear, and "Turtle Food" (broken bits of balloons). In

2021, it all went on display at the Australian National Maritime Museum in Sydney. She then created a second version, to display in Queensland.

A phenomenon that strikes Marina as particularly unsettling is the quantity of brand-new stuff—often not even out of its box yet—that people and businesses leave out on the street. After picking up a few loads of these boxes, she opened the Wasted Opportunity Shop. There were TVs, even. She sold everything, and donated the money to a local repair shop, with the idea of promoting the habit of fixing versus tossing.

In 2020, she was finally able to give up cleaning houses, which was the side gig that had allowed her to afford making art all these years. There is not a major market for waterlogged, foul-smelling clothes or a sculpture composed of abandoned beach pails. Not even for her *Dispensable Dispenser,* a vending machine selling corks, colored plastic, and tiny plastic bottles. But she makes money putting together educational exhibits, working with cities and towns to do thought-provoking installations and government-sponsored shows.

But money—or the lack of it—is not stopping her. Her current favorite project is a sculpture she made of one hundred bird wings—real bird wings. These are shearwater birds, from Tasmania, which are dying off because of all the plastic they are ingesting.

Her ultimate dream is to run out of art supplies.

FACT: In 1992, twenty-eight thousand (or so) rubber duckies and other bath toys were dumped into the sea when a shipping container leaving Hong Kong went overboard. The bath toys have been drifting all over the world in the decades since, serving as unintentional educators about the ocean's currents. Members of the "Friendly Floatees," a name given to this plastic armada, have been discovered on the beaches of Hawaii, Alaska, South America, Australia, the Pacific Northwest, and even on the Arctic ice. Some two hundred duckies are still circulating in the currents of the North Pacific Subtropical Gyre, providing scientists with new information about what is now known as the Great Pacific Garbage Patch. The bath toys have even become the subject of a book called *Moby-Duck.*

Leah Thomas

Founder of

Intersectional Environmentalist

Bringing justice to the environmental movement

I AM ODDLY GOOD AT: Conflict resolution. I like to calm people down.

I AM ODDLY BAD AT: cleaning

MY GREATEST FEAR: The deep ocean. It freaks me out.

A GUILTY PLEASURE: *Real Housewives of Atlanta* or *Potomac* (Leah and Lisa Jackson, another of the "girls who green the world," would be friends)

THE TRAIT I MOST DEPLORE IN MYSELF: I can be overly perfectionistic.

A WORD OR PHRASE I MOST OVERUSE: "literally"

A HABIT I'M TRYING TO GIVE UP: meat

SOMETHING I USED TO DO BEFORE I REALIZED HOW BAD IT WAS FOR THE ENVIRONMENT: buy fast fashion

Leah Thomas is the face of new environmentalism. She found her activist voice on a summer day in 2014. She was home from college, just out of the shower on a Saturday, when her text screen started blowing up. A few miles away in Ferguson, Missouri, a Black teen had been killed. By now the case is famous: eighteen-year-old Michael Brown, unarmed, was shot multiple times by a police officer. His death set off a wave of protests; the National Guard was sent in to quell the violence, and a new front in our country's race reckoning opened.

Leah didn't know Michael, "but he was just a few friends circles away." That proximity left her reeling. She spent the summer struggling with her feelings and protesting, but come September, she headed back to Chapman University in Southern California. While she deciphered the fine print of the Clean Air Act and Clean Water Act in class—she was an environmental science major—her sister and friends in Missouri were choking on tear gas, fighting for justice. Leah struggled to hold these realities, the "juxtaposition of laws that are supposed to be protecting people, and my community burning down because of injustice."

While she deciphered the fine print of the Clean Air Act and Clean Water Act, her sister and friends in Missouri were choking on tear gas, fighting for justice.

She now refers to the events in Ferguson as "my identity wake-up." She was forced to confront her Blackness and her environmentalism concurrently. These are not identities that are easy to hold together. She wondered, "Why doesn't my program have any environmental justice requirements? Why don't I have any environmental science professors that look like me?" She was the only Black environmental science major that year.

Still grappling, she graduated and applied for a job in communications at Patagonia, a pioneer of corporate environmental-mindedness.

She didn't get the job. Instead of wallowing, she focused on her resume. Bulking it out, that is. This meant taking a position at a (then) small environmental company, Ecos, handling social media and brand partnerships. Ecos makes eco-safe laundry detergent and other soaps. Leah had a knack for writing about the products, and she was skilled at creating graphics and forging connections. A year later, she reapplied to Patagonia with her jacked resume. They hired her.

Then, in March 2020, the COVID-19 pandemic hit. With whole cities shuttering and the economy in free fall, she was let go. The furlough was devastating.

But her distress was quickly thrown into perspective. On May 25, 2020, a police officer in Minneapolis pinned a Black man named George Floyd to the ground, cutting off his airway for more than eight minutes and forty-six seconds. The terrible event was recorded, Floyd died, and Leah was instantly transported back to Ferguson. "How can we work to save the earth, yet continually forsake Black and brown people? How can we need clean air and water but allow toxic street scenes daily?" she asked.

On her Instagram @greengirlleah, she went public with her fears, posting a simple graphic reading "Environmentalists for Black Lives Matter" followed by an Intersectional Environmentalist Pledge that she created, one tenet of which read "I will not remain silent during pivotal political and cultural moments that impact BIPOC communities." Her plan then and now is to expand an environmental movement that has been distressingly narrow. Saving trees, open spaces, and whales, and preserving pristine mountain lakes and national parks for recreation are all nice-to-haves. But these fights miss a critical reality: the greater impacts of environmental hazards on marginalized communities. An EPA study indicated that people of color are much more likely to live near polluters and breathe polluted air, stating specifically that "results at national, state, and county scales all indicate that non-Whites tend to be burdened disproportionately to Whites."

Ever wonder why so much low-income housing sits in flood zones?

"Environmental activists talk often about a hypothetical climate crisis that will come years and years from now. But they ignore that the climate crisis is *already* here for poor people and people of color," Leah said. She has gathered the courage to say, "Okay, all these species are endangered, but Black people are also endangered."

Her words instantly hit a nerve, going viral, grabbing fifty thousand likes and shares in a few days. Two weeks on, her followership of thirteen thousand had jumped to over a hundred thousand. Clearly, what she had to say, others were looking to hear. Today she has a quarter of a million followers.

For Leah, this was the start of a movement. In this way—putting justice into the eco-mix—she's giving voice to next-wave environmentalism.

Days after her viral post, she pulled together a diverse team of young leaders and, within a week, launched the site Intersectional Environmentalist (IE), a media and resource platform dedicated to this new environmentalism. The mission: to promote an inclusive form of environmentalism that advocates for the protection of all people and the planet. The primary objective is education. They provide mentorship, workshops, grants, toolkits, and research. "We don't think having a college degree should be the only way to get accessible climate info," she said. The materials on the site, she has heard, have already been incorporated into school courses and curricula—that's the goal. In the summer of 2021, IE launched a free lecture series on environmental justice.

This endeavor is not Leah's first tangle with racial politics. She was raised by two Black parents in what was initially a mixed-race Saint Louis suburb. Then her white neighbors, one by one, left for more homogenous suburbs. Her parents were not immune to wanting the best schools for their kids; that required sending Leah thirty minutes away to a private school, which she attended on scholarship and where she was one of very few Black students. "I had to leave my community in order to have access to the right education, nature, green spaces, clean air," she said. It's a history that dovetails with her mission.

Her visibility and network have grown at warp speed. In just a year, she has been profiled in *National Geographic, W* magazine, and *Harper's Bazaar,* and on BuzzFeed. She also graced the cover of *Outside* magazine. In January 2021, she was featured in a Super Bowl ad for Logitech—as one of their model "genre breakers." Soon after President Biden was elected, she snagged an Instagram Live interview with his new deputy national climate adviser, Ali Zaidi. On the heels of that, she interviewed former vice president Al Gore, who, at seventy-three, is still a leading progressive thinker on climate. He encourages young activists to pressure leaders to act for climate justice.

If you think Leah was doing a little dance, think again. It was Gore who gushed like a fangirl.

> **IDEA:** "A lot of times when people talk about environmental justice, they go back to the 1970s or '60s. But I think about the slave quarters. I think about people who got the worst food, the worst healthcare, the worst treatment, and then when freed, were given lands that were eventually surrounded by things like petrochemical industries. The idea of killing Black people or Indigenous people, all of that has a long, long history that is centered on capitalism and the extraction of our land and our labor in this country."
> —Elizabeth Yeampierre, Climate Justice Alliance

FACT: Climate change will cause the most economic harm in the nation's poorest counties; many of those places, like Zavala County, Texas, and Wilkinson County, Mississippi, are home to mostly people of color.

V

Screw Fossil Fuels

Mary Anne Hitt

Senior Director of

Climate Imperative at Energy Innovation:
Policy and Technology LLC

and National Director of Campaigns,

the Sierra Club

Closing down coal—forever

I AM ODDLY GOOD AT: making music and singing—stuff like Lucinda Williams and other Americana singer-songwriters

I AM ODDLY BAD AT: competitive sports

MY GREATEST FEAR: something happening to my family

THE TRAIT I MOST DEPLORE IN MYSELF: I don't get my daughter outside enough. It's so easy to get sucked into your screen.

AN OCCASION WHEN I LIE: promising my daughter everything is going to be okay

A WORD OR PHRASE I MOST OVERUSE: "excellent"

A HABIT I'M TRYING TO GIVE UP: procrastinating

SOMETHING I USED TO DO BEFORE I REALIZED HOW BAD IT WAS FOR THE ENVIRONMENT: Drive a very polluting '66 Mustang convertible. It was a cool car for a high schooler.

In the mid-1980s, red spruce and sugar maples in the highest reaches of Great Smoky Mountains National Park started looking like skeletons. The hallmark trees of America's most visited national park were being decimated by a mysterious force. Mary Anne Hitt remembers lying in her childhood bed, worrying about the trees, but more about her dad. He was chief scientist for the national park. When he suggested that something called acid rain was killing trees, government and coal industry officials threw the proverbial acid back in his face.

Nobody in positions of power in Tennessee wanted to hear that the biggest moneymaker in the state—coal plants—were harmful. But they were. When coal is burned to produce electricity, sulfur oxides are released, which react with oxygen in the air, which makes contact with water molecules in the atmosphere, producing acidic pollutants. This material then falls from the sky, stripping leaves and soil of nutrients, leaving majestic trees brown and shriveled.

Mary Anne's environmental and political education began at her father's knee. Forty years later, she is now leading the crusade he helped begin . . . and winning. By 2030, Mary Anne will have forced the closure of some 339 coal plants.

> *By 2030, Mary Anne will have forced the closure of some 339 coal plants.*

Her rise through the environmental movement was swift. By her late twenties, she was head of a nonprofit called Appalachian Voices, working furiously to keep coal mining companies from blowing the tops off any more mountains in the area. That was in 2007. Then as now, "mountaintop removal mining" was an incredibly popular method of mining coal because it exposes the layers of coal deposits in a way that makes them easy to reach—that is, once a peak lies crumbled in a valley, the exposed swath of coal is ripe for the pickin'. And after coal has been extracted from one section, another section is blown up to expose yet more coal.

Mary Anne wasn't just offended that the landscape that had brought her parents to settle in Tennessee was being destroyed. The process was hazardous on multiple levels. Silica particles released in the mining were being linked to cancer. The explosions also released mercury, a neurotoxin, which ends up in water and then fish and then human mouths. And, the real kicker, when coal is burned, of all fossil fuels, it's the worst emitter of carbon dioxide.

But the coal industry was hard to slow down back then. President George W. Bush made it his business to advance the construction of two hundred new coal-fired power plants during his two terms. Mary Anne remembers thinking, "Someone has got to stop this," and then, after looking around her, seeing no hands raised, she realized, "Oh, that someone is going to be me."

It wasn't the first time she had that revelation. Sophomore year at the University of Tennessee, she plopped down in a chair in a chaotic meeting room, waiting for the environmental club's first meeting to come to order. Twenty or so students had gathered and were waiting with her. "Someone will be right here to get us organized," Mary Anne thought. "Whoever is in charge is running late." But no one showed up to get anything going. Five more minutes passed, and still no chairperson or adviser. So Mary

Anne pushed out of her chair, stood in front of the group, and began to lead. She followed advice she now frequently gives to young people: If you are thinking somebody should do something, that somebody is probably going to be you.

If you are thinking somebody should do something, that somebody is probably going to be you.

Regarding those two hundred new planned coal plants during the Bush era—Mary Anne appointed herself chief agitator. She scoped out her allies and discovered that the Sierra Club was already elbow-deep in the matter. So she decided to join them. Her partner-in-interference, Bruce Nilles, showed her how to energize a grassroots army in every state. They would poke holes in coal plant building permits, storm into hearings, hound politicians, and wave signs in front of passersby. They called their campaign Beyond Coal.

Mary Anne and Bruce decided to fight every single new plant, no matter the size. "We knew anything built was going to lead to massive growth in climate destruction," she said. "And every [plant] is in somebody's backyard."

The "scrappy" grassroots effort required 24/7 vigilance. A massive spreadsheet was their best weapon. They listed every single project, with the stage of development, permit status, and upcoming decision dates. Each phase demanded discrete actions. That's because full approval to build a plant involves a dozen or more permits. There are zoning requirements, Clean Air Act and water regulations. For each of these, there are public comment periods, approval processes. If Mary Anne and her team could interfere with any of these steps along the way, they might derail the whole process. But if they missed any of those "comment" periods, no challenge would stop the construction. They had to stay on their toes.

They became expert blockers. So expert that they managed to keep 184 of those 200 slated plants from ever breaking ground. Mary Anne is still sore about one that got away, in West Virginia, which is where she lives. "You learn a lot from your losses."

But mostly she won, again and again and again.

Success juiced her ambition. "Why stop with newly planned projects?" Mary Anne thought. There were 530 coal plants already online, puffing carbon dioxide. Why not go after them, too? On average, coal plants are forty years old. Old plants need upgrades to comply with regulations. Upgrades require approvals and permits. Approvals and permits are ambrosia for agitators like Mary Anne.

The plants were falling like flies: the Eddystone Generating Station in Pennsylvania. Big Brown Power Plant in Texas. Dolet Hills in Louisiana. The Fisk and Crawford plants in Chicago. The Sierra Club had hundreds of partner organizations to help them, and they had momentum on their side because the economics of energy were changing. Natural gas was now cheaper than coal. The price of renewables like wind and solar were dropping fast, too. The "cheap" economics of coal was crumbling.

But then came a new president. It was 2017, and Mary Anne was at her desk working while CNN prattled on in the background. She turned toward the screen just as the Environmental Protection Agency (EPA) head Scott Pruitt and President Trump approached a podium. She moved closer to the TV. The president was pleased to announce that he'd just pulled the US out of the Paris Agreement, the world's best cooperative plan to delay or even solve climate change. He also wanted to inform viewers that US coal was back. Big-time.

Mary Anne eyed her daughter coloring on the bed behind her. Then she burst into tears. She couldn't help but feel a "great foreboding" about her daughter's future.

But moments later, she felt oddly powerful. Confident. She recognized that she knew way more about the dynamics around coal than these politicians ever would, and how the process of bringing plants online works. Everything happens at the state and local levels, so the federal government didn't actually have the power to bring back coal.

She knew way more about the dynamics around coal than these politicians ever would.

She and the Sierra Club went back to the spreadsheets, and filing lawsuits, obstructing progress, and closing more and more plants. In 2020, they closed eight plants, their best year ever.

A decade ago, half of America's energy came from coal. Coal was our biggest source of greenhouse gas emissions, too. Today less than a quarter of America's energy comes from coal. The writing is on the wall. Coal is going down.

The next hurdle is: What replaces coal? The fossil fuel industry wants it to be natural gas. Environmentalists want renewable energy like wind and solar. There's also the question of jobs. All those coal miners need to earn a living, but Mary Anne doesn't want them running to natural gas's fracking operations to get them. These new goals require new spreadsheets.

Mary Anne has never lacked for a can-do attitude. In 2021, in fact, she decided to jump jobs, to expand beyond closing down coal to closing down all fossil fuels. She joined her same Sierra Club co-conspirator Bruce at a policy outfit focused on implementing change at the government level. Their mission is to make the most impact in the shortest amount of time on emissions that cause climate change. She knows that pressure, applied correctly, works, no matter the size of the enemy. "I have had this incredible privilege to watch David beat Goliath hundreds of times." In this fight, she will never lack for Goliaths. More are out there, and she is coming for them.

> **FACT:** Coal-fired power plants release more greenhouse gases per unit of energy produced than any other electricity source.

> **FACT:** After a coal plant closure, some of the worst toxic pollutants disappear from the air within days. But carbon dioxide is not among them. It can linger in the atmosphere for hundreds of years, capturing heat and intensifying global warming all the while.

How to Make an Impact on Cutting Fossil Fuels (from Mary Anne Hitt, who has closed 339 coal plants)

Writing skillfully will serve you well on any path you take to fight climate change. From opinion pieces to tweets to grant proposals, I rely on my writing skills daily. And as a manager, having staff who can write well is something I value highly. Words have power, and they are an important tool.

People often feel powerless imagining that all the "important" decisions are happening in Washington, DC, or even the state capitol far away. Forget that. Wherever you live, there are important decisions being made about climate change. Wherever you live, your voice matters.

Electricity and transportation—two of the biggest consumers of fossil fuel and sources of climate change—are operated at the state level. Every year, state legislators are making big decisions about both. Those people, or their staff, are accessible. They are not celebrities. You can easily meet with them, call them, and write them letters. Learn the issues. Then make yourself heard.

Create the change you want to see in the world. Instead of griping, bring to life examples like community gardens or a more accessible bike path.

When you want to push for change, identify what you want and who can give it to you. Be as specific as possible about both. The decision-maker shouldn't just be a government agency or business or organization, but a specific person who can deliver the result you want. You can then build a campaign around whatever it takes to move that person toward your goal.

If you can't figure out where to plug in to fight fossil fuels, look to successful organizations running grassroots efforts, including 350.org, the Sunrise Movement, the Sierra Club, Greenpeace, and myriad local organizations.

Just get started. You don't need to become a bit more of an expert or earn a degree or get just a little more up to speed. . . . You are enough right now. Whatever you have to contribute is enough. Just look at Greta and the Sunrise Movement for inspiration on that.

Lynn Jurich

Cofounder and Chief Executive Officer of

Sunrun

Leading the rooftop solar revolution . . .
500,000 homes so far

I AM ODDLY GOOD AT: finding the most efficient way to do something

I AM ODDLY BAD AT: being patient

MY FAVORITE SNACK: potato chips

AN UNUSUAL WORK HABIT: starting staff meetings with a Japanese tea ceremony

HOW I DE-STRESS: daily meditation

I ADMIRE: Lucille Ball

SOMETHING INTERESTING YOU'D FIND ON MY DESK: a signed photo of Roger Federer

IF I COULD CHANGE ONE HUMAN BEHAVIOR TO SAVE THE PLANET, IT WOULD BE: ditch air-conditioning

Today the word "solar" is buzzy. If you live in a city, you've probably parked under a solar array in the last ten days; you probably know at least one person with a plug-in car who invested in solar panels to charge it. But in early 2007, when Lynn Jurich was trying to get homeowners to switch from fossil fuels to solar power, the concept was still pretty far-out and, worse, pricey. Most Saturdays she'd find herself at a dusty county fair or farmers' market, sitting behind an off-balance card table, side-eyeing a stack of flyers nobody wanted. Everyone around her was on the hunt for smooth-skinned zucchinis and portly pumpkins, and she was peddling energy from the sun. She'd wipe the sweat off her lip and try to remember why she'd given up her investment job, private jets, and expense-account dinners. Then someone would accidentally pass her janky stand, and Lynn would pop out of her chair, shove a flyer into their hand, and say, "Hey, how much do you spend on your energy bill monthly?"

It would have been pride-swallowing sales work if it hadn't been saving the planet.

Her novel sales pitch went something like this: "I don't want to sell you solar panels. I want you to essentially rent them from me. My company, Sunrun, makes it easy. Our technicians just pull up to your house, install a roof's worth of panels, handle future upkeep, and bill you monthly for the service. And, to make it affordable, you just need to sign a twenty-year contract."

It all sounded reasonable and cool—"Solar as a service!"—until she got to that last line. That was about when people walked away with a snort and wave. Most marriages don't last twenty years. Invest in a solar package that lasts that long? Nah.

Most marriages don't last twenty years.
Invest in a solar package that lasts that long? Nah.

Still, Lynn had been born to sell. She knew she was early-to-market and had to win over hearts and minds with a bulletproof pitch. She adjusted her spiel. After a year of glad-handing amidst the veggies and farm animals, she'd signed up a thousand customers. It was a start.

Founding Sunrun had always been a gamble. Most of Lynn's peers from Stanford business school had gone in for a "sure thing"—banking or building apps. Lynn had always had bigger plans after graduation—that is, fundamental societal change.

With this on her mind, a conversation with an environmentalist classmate with a solar agenda had felt like seriously good karma. They were definitely speaking the same language about what motivated them, and how they might go about starting their own business. Each thought the other was the ideal business partner. In no time, she and Ed shook hands as cofounders.

It was a bumpy year one. Not a lot of money was coming in, and at home, Lynn's husband was in start-up mode, too. The couple quickly recognized that two risky start-ups in one household would never work. They agreed that "whoever had the best idea would go first and the other would get a regular job." Lynn won that test, too.

In her blue, down puff coat and blond ponytail, she gives off a very low-key CEO vibe. Don't be fooled. She's never been low-key, not even as a kid. While her dad had extracted rotten molars (dentist) and her mom had processed claims for the Social Security Administration, Lynn had made to-do lists. Here's a sample: "inventing, practice ballet, practice piano, singing, read the dictionary."

You don't become CEO of America's largest rooftop solar installer by examining the folds in your belly button.

At college applications time, her parents wanted her at the University of Washington. Lynn wanted more. She got into Stanford and then took full advantage, pursuing every STEM subject possible. A college summer program in China made a lasting impact—the polluted air turned white face masks gray within hours. "Clean air should be a right," she thought.

After graduating, she joined a private-equity investment firm, part of a prestigious industry with almost no women. Her job revolved around sweet-talking CEOs—often starting with a cold call—into hiring her firm. She kept a running list of crafty ways of getting CEOs' ears. "Like, become friends with their assistant so you can get a seat on the airplane next to them. Or never approach somebody on a Monday. Or learning which conferences they're going to," and then bumping into them there.

In Sunrun's early days, those cold-calling skills were a secret weapon. She knew little about the electrical power infrastructure, the grid, or solar panels. To get smart, she mined the entire Stanford alumni database, searching for the pros in the field. They called her back and mansplained why Sunrun had no chance. "They'd say, 'There are lots of sophisticated people working on this stuff. Go home, little girl.'" Lynn was good at ignoring the naysayers.

Today she and her team have installed solar on five hundred thousand

homes, and they have raised $9 billion in capital. In 2020, Lynn earned the *New York Times* headline SHE'S TAKING ON ELON MUSK ON SOLAR. AND WINNING. Tesla, her biggest competitor, has tried everything to knock Sunrun off its pedestal, including buying other solar start-ups. But Sunrun is playing its own game, and has acquired the $3.2 billion, four-thousand-person Vivint Solar to grow even faster.

> *Tesla, her biggest competitor, has tried everything to knock Sunrun off its pedestal.*

Every step has been a fight. Tesla is just the latest in a long line of almost-derailments. Take September 29, 2008, when, in six and a half frantic hours, $1.2 trillion vanished from the US stock market. Banks were failing, Congress was paralyzed, and the economy imploded. Sustainability, climate change, and home improvement fell off everybody's to-do list. The solar market was sunk. Sunrun survived, but disaster struck again in 2011, when a government program giving 30 percent cash rebates as an incentive to encourage converting to solar was canned due to budget woes. A tax benefit cancellation was also announced, though not to take effect immediately. Sales went from "a hundred new customers a month to just nine," Lynn said. "We thought 'Do we have to shut the business down?'"

Sunrun survived that, too. Then Lynn celebrated her thirty-fifth birthday and, blowing out candles, realized two things at once: she wanted to have a baby before her body said, "Too late, lady," AND it was time to do an Initial Public Offering (IPO) and get on the stock exchange. Sunrun needed an infusion of cash to keep competing and growing. Somehow, milk-stained and deprived of sleep, she managed both at the same time.

Lynn ultimately recruited her mom to help as the travel and pressure increased. She raced from city to city to sell the Sunrun story to investors, basically living in hotels with her mom, baby, and a breast pump, and working in boardrooms with bankers, lawyers, and her executive team. Sometimes she was in between, in a bathroom stall pumping breast milk. And sometimes the bankers—the ones who understood the family-job juggle—would ferry the milk back to Lynn's baby. Happily, on the day Sunrun debuted on the Nasdaq exchange and Lynn got to ring the opening bell, her mom and daughter were right beside her, "three generations of Jurich women."

Lynn sometimes swigs NyQuil to fall asleep, due to stress. But that's because this work is mission-critical. Energy accounts for 80 percent of carbon emissions. "You have to solve energy to solve climate," she said. Solar is growing, yet still provides just about 2 percent of US electricity. But in California, that number is 12 percent. Hawaii has 30 percent adoption. Battery technology is changing the solar game, because the energy can be stored for use when the sun is down, or saved and sold to the grid when the rays are producing more than one house needs. That's huge. As of 2019, solar energy is cheaper than fossil fuels. Massive opportunity awaits.

"You have to solve energy to solve climate."

FACT: The US Bureau of Labor Statistics estimates that "wind turbine service technician" will be the fastest-growing job between 2019 and 2029, with a median annual wage over $42,000. "Solar photovoltaic installer," a fancy term for a rooftop panel installer and upkeeper, will be the third-fastest-growing occupation.

FACT: Since 2010, the cost of residential solar has plummeted 65 percent. There is an expectation of a 17 percent further reduction by 2025. Solar prices have "dropped off a cliff and sunk to the bottom of the sea," as a *CleanTechnica* news story puts it.

Kathy Hannun

Cofounder and President of

Dandelion Energy

Tapping Earth's furnace

I AM ODDLY GOOD AT: finding four-leaf clovers

I AM ODDLY BAD AT: spatially orienting myself in unfamiliar places

MY GREATEST FEAR: I will be an old woman and realize I just lived a life without enjoyment and appreciation for the day-to-day.

A GUILTY PLEASURE: *The Great British Bake Off.* I don't even like baking, or eat many baked goods. . . .

THE TRAIT I MOST DEPLORE IN MYSELF: wish I didn't sunburn so easily

AN OCCASION WHEN I LIE: The founder of a company we were hoping to partner with suggested an idea for my company. It was a terrible idea—unrealistic, possibly not even physically possible. I responded with a polite "Interesting idea. I will look into it!" I certainly wasn't planning to look into it.

A TIME I'D RATHER NOT REMEMBER: a terrible breakup right when I graduated from college and then immediately went to Mexico for an internship where no one spoke English or Spanish (the language was an indigenous one)

MY GREATEST ACHIEVEMENT: marrying my husband, Awni

Kathy Hannun doesn't like the way we warm our houses. It makes no sense. Gas-filled tanks in basements attached to heated boxes and tubes? Fire hazard. Carbon monoxide hazard. Pollution hazard! Kathy is pretty sure humans in 2123 will look back at our furnace-based heating habits of today and think "What a bunch of numbskulls."

Already, Kathy knows there's a better way—geothermal energy. The word "geothermal" sounds complicated, but it's actually really basic: the earth's temperature just below the surface crust never changes. Dig down ten feet, and the temperature will be 55 degrees. On a 90-degree sweltering August day—55 degrees. In a blinding snow blizzard—yep, 55 degrees. Kathy's company, Dandelion Energy, taps that warmth stored in the ground to heat homes.

How'd she come to take on this long-known-but-little-implemented idea back in 2017? Well, it was a journey . . .

Kathy is the daughter of a powerful, independent-minded woman who herself is the daughter of a powerful, independent-minded woman. Kathy owes much to her maternal lineage. Her grandmother suffered through a long and exhausting labor giving birth to her mom. When the doctor pulled out the baby, umbilical cord not yet clipped, he huffed, "All that work for a girl." Kathy's grandma resolved to make sure her girl would "defy that comment."

She did. Kathy's mom became the only fertility doctor and obstetrician in tiny Dover, New Hampshire, where Kathy grew up, the kind of place where the bank teller gives you cash even when you've forgotten your ID, because you look just like your mom. (This happened.) Kathy's mom was a local hero, personally responsible for delivering all the town's babies. She raised Kathy to be the same kind of indispensable person.

First, Kathy tried medicine. It was familiar; from her mom, she understood its rewards. But all that memorization—learning the two hundred and six bones in the skeleton—was not her forte. Stanford let Kathy jump to a new major: engineering. This clicked. She loved tackling big systemic problems and figuring out how to fix them.

After graduation in 2008, she thought she'd definitely find work in her field. But with zero relevant experience, she found zero jobs. One year later, she was still unemployed and miserable. Her cousin told her about an opening at one of the world's most exciting companies—Google. Unfortunately, the position was in customer support for the advertising department. Could a job get any duller? What did ad support have to do with design, engines, machines, structures? But, desperate for a paycheck, Kathy signed on. All day, she coded email inquiries so they would return the correct automatic response. It was "humans doing a job a computer could do," as she described it.

As boring as this was, she says it was the right path. "I tell graduates, 'Don't wait for the perfect job. Just take one that moves you in the direction you want to go.'"

To stay sharp, she enrolled in nighttime computer science courses at Stanford. Google has the perk of covering continuing education for employees. "Pretty quickly I could have written the code to replace myself in my job," she said. She eventually earned a master's in theoretical computer science.

After hopping around to a few more unchallenging posts at Google, her persistence paid off. A marketing job opened at Google X, the super-secretive group pursuing "moonshots" like self-driving cars and flying delivery drones. She got hired. It still wasn't exactly the role she wanted but was a step closer. She initially produced Google X's glitzy events. Google cofounder Sergey Brin's skydive at the Google Glass unveiling? That was

Kathy's doing. But soon she was promoted to the rapid-evaluation squad, who decide which of Google X's zillions of ideas to pursue. Ding. Driver's seat.

First she latched on to a technology to turn seawater into fuel. She invited the scientist to give a talk to her colleagues at Google X. She analyzed the chemistry and was convinced seawater had real potential as an energy source that could fuel jets and ships. She decided to throw herself into research, convinced the investment of her time and energy was worth it. But what if she was wrong? Doubt plagued her. Her colleagues were former CEOs. They seemed so sure of everything. But she felt like an impostor pretending to be sure of herself.

She didn't know yet that leading meant risking failure all the time. The CEOs were just more experienced at failing than she was.

The CEOs were just more
experienced at failing than she was.

As it happened, the water technology project hit a dead end, as experiments often do. But Kathy soon found herself distracted by another new energy project being proposed to Google X: geothermal heat pumps, a one-hundred-sixty-year-old idea reconfigured for the modern age.

As with the seawater project, Kathy spent long days and nights trying to figure out the project's fatal flaws, the reasons why it wouldn't work, wouldn't be practical, couldn't be duplicated around the world.

But she never found them. Instead, she fell hard for the idea. It was just too astonishing: research showed that the earth contained enough heat to warm not only every building on earth but every building that will ever exist, for all time. Why had this tech ever been overlooked?

To truly appreciate the magical properties of geothermal energy, you need to understand how a typical home is heated today—that is, the furnace. Your furnace is likely hiding in your basement—waiting for that moment when your house hits 67 degrees, and then it kicks on. That revving sound you hear (and sometimes feel under your feet), that's the furnace releasing gas, which it then burns—producing heat energy. This heated air gets pushed into vents and out to you. It's a messy process that emits a lot of carbon into the atmosphere. Simply cooling, heating, and powering households puts off roughly 20 percent of energy-related greenhouse gas emissions, a 2020 Proceedings of the National Academy of Sciences study of the US carbon footprint found.

Geothermal energy is the opposite of messy.

To access the earth's heat, geothermal systems like Kathy's use U-shaped pipes buried in a house's yard. Each end connects to a heat pump in the house. Water is run underground in a constant loop through the pipes. The water, which is warmed up by exposure to the earth's natural heat while flowing through the deeply buried pipes, enters a concentrator (run by electricity) that intensifies the heat. This heat energy then warms air, which comes through vents in the house to make happy, warm feet.

Nothing in the geothermal system is a pollutant. If you think of it in terms of carbon swaps, for every house with a geothermal system, it's the equivalent of eighteen cars coming off the road (over a twenty-five-year period). Install geothermal systems in a hundred homes, and say sayonara to the equivalent of eighteen hundred carbon-spewing cars. The math gets exciting fast.

Kathy saw the potential of geothermal power reaching the masses. But one of the obstacles standing in the way of that vision was how difficult it was to put ground loops in people's yards. Installing ground loops entailed using drills mounted on monster trucks. The process had the potential to turn a yard into a pool-sized mud pit—if the truck could even get into the yard in the first place. Most yards were just too small for these trucks to fit at all.

Before Google X would believe it was backing a viable idea, Kathy had to resolve this installation hurdle. A mud pit is not what homeowners want, even in exchange for cheap, renewable heating. . . .

Kathy knew there had to be an easier way to install pipe underground. Her team brainstormed. No wacky idea was rejected. They tried modifying a jackhammer that could burrow itself in the ground like a "mechanical mole": a bust. They considered freezing the ground with liquid nitrogen and chipping the soil away with a hammer: another bust. They used a high-pressure water jet to obliterate the ground at rocket speeds: bust number three.

But then they discovered the elegant solution of using a drill that could liquefy the ground using sonic vibration, called sonic drilling technology. By resonating the soil particles so they behaved more like a liquid than solid ground, the drilling team could just slip the drill string right into the ground. They designed a suite of drilling equipment that was small and trim so it could fit into those small yards that were way too constrained to fit a typical truck-mounted rig. And the team invested in equipment to process all the mud and water that came out of the hole so it didn't mess up the yard. A modest suburban yard could be barbecue-bash-ready the day after an install.

Kathy was certain that her low-impact system would thrill customers. But she also knew she'd been in a research bubble for years and had no idea what consumers would go for. So, Kathy hired market researchers and sent them into the field to interview potential customers. How much would you pay? What are your concerns about geothermal? Are you ready to sign up? She tagged along to learn but kept quiet.

Their reactions reassured her. The only hesitation consumers had: big up-front costs. But Kathy had anticipated this and had a clever offer. What if Dandelion loaned customers the money for installation? Customers would then pay the loan off in small monthly installments. The best news: those payments, plus the monthly geothermal bill, would still be cheaper than using oil or gas.

All seemed rosy. She'd found an idea that Google X could throw its muscle behind. Finally. But when she put her market researchers up in front of the Google X team to present their conclusions, it was as if they had been listening to entirely different customers. The takeaway, they said, was that there was no market for geothermal. This was a dead-letter idea. Going nowhere.

Kathy was shocked. Had she made the oldest mistake in the book? Was she an inventor overly attached to an idea, blinded by her desire to make it work? Had she lost all credibility inside the office?

Had she made the oldest mistake in the book? Was she an inventor overly attached to an idea, blinded by her desire to make it work?

Maybe. But her idea was smart. Her technology was good. Her timing was right. She knew it. She couldn't give up now. Remember her powerful, independent-minded maternal lineage? She recognized that the only way to know if her instincts were right was to start selling geothermal systems.

She was going out on her own. She started in upstate New York. With the very cold winters there, people spend heavily on home heat. She named her new company after dandelions because the simple yellow flowers grow everywhere, a happy weed, nothing special about them. She felt the same would be true for her geothermal systems—they'd be ubiquitous.

With hustle and a great pitch, she secured funding. With funding, she bought trucks and warehouses, then hired and trained installers. She even got certified as an installer. (Don't picture her in steel-toed boots, riding a jackhammer; she left that to the pros, but she wanted to know exactly how the job was done so she could jump in when trouble cropped up.)

By December 2020, five hundred homes were being heated by Dandelion geothermal energy in New York State. That number doubled in 2021, and Kathy predicts that number will double again in 2022. They have expanded to Connecticut. Dandelion's goal is to ramp up to ten thousand installations per year, and with $30 million just invested by Bill Gates, the company is off and running.

Not all her instincts were right. She hired the wrong help at first. She probably waited too long to leave Google X. She got pregnant in the middle of her biggest round of fundraising and had to wear baggy clothes to all her interviews, because she was pretty sure (sadly) that men would not want to loan money to a new mom.

But she was right about the technology and consumer adoption. The geothermal homes emit 80 percent less greenhouse gases than furnace-heated homes. People see and love the cost savings. She's making a difference. On February 4, 2020, Kathy was snug in her seat in the House Chamber in the US Capitol. Beside her was New York Congressman Paul Tonko, who had brought her as his guest to the State of the Union address. She was there to represent the future of energy.

FACT: Installing a single geothermal unit is the environmental equivalent of planting seven hundred fifty trees, according to the Ecology Action Center.

Your Vote Matters Most

No amount of composting, toting reusable bags to the grocery store, or even banning plastic bags in every shop in your town will have nearly as much impact as electing candidates who will move us off fossil fuels. We need to cut use and production at scale, which demands that corporations change their ways. This starts with policy change. Corporations and municipalities act when regulations provide strict caps on fossil fuel emissions or financially incentivize the move to renewable energy like geothermal or solar.

If you are too young to vote, you can still influence who gets elected. First, talk to your parents, teachers, and other grown-ups in your life about why we must act now, which includes them going out to vote. Research who the pro-environment candidates are at every level of government, from your city leadership to state officials to US congressional representatives. Organizations like the League of Conservation Voters offer "green" scorecards on candidates. You can volunteer for their campaigns, work for their phone banks, knock on doors, create social media campaigns on their behalf, and work at the polls.

Nicole Poindexter

Founder and Chief Executive Officer of

Energicity Corp

Lighting up West Africa

I AM ODDLY GOOD AT: making smoothies

I AM ODDLY BAD AT: catching balls

MY GREATEST FEAR: not healing the planet (and rodents)

A GUILTY PLEASURE: white cake cupcakes with buttercream icing, and barbecue brisket

THE TRAIT I MOST DEPLORE IN MYSELF: deploring anything about myself

AN OCCASION WHEN I LIE: when I'm late

A WORD OR PHRASE I MOST OVERUSE: "That said . . ."

A HABIT I'M TRYING TO GIVE UP: action without purpose and purpose without action

SOMETHING I USED TO DO BEFORE I REALIZED HOW BAD IT WAS FOR THE ENVIRONMENT: own a car

FACT: There are as many people living without power today as there were when Thomas Edison lit the first light bulb. More than half are in sub-Saharan Africa.

Nicole Poindexter remembers the first time she heard about Ghana's electricity problems. It was 2012, and she was using her degrees from Harvard and Yale to work for a software company, helping consumers around the world learn to save energy, particularly electricity. The reason was simple: the less energy we waste, the better off our planet and our wallets are. But in Ghana, in West Africa, waste was not a problem. To waste, you have to have an abundance of something. In Ghana, there was never enough electricity to go around. According to Nicole's friend Kofi, who lived in Ghana, the lights were constantly flickering. They could go off for hours at a time, with no notice. There was a term for the phenomenon—dum/sor, which translates to off/on. In reality, it was mostly dum . . . dum . . . dum . . . dum. Every day.

Imagine trying to study for a test with no Wi-Fi or light. Imagine trying to operate on a patient. . . .

And it wasn't just Ghana, Nicole learned. Six hundred million people across Africa still live with no electricity.

This needed immediate attention. This needed a whip-smart, well-trained problem solver. A trailblazer. Nicole wrote to her friend Kofi, "What would you think if I were to tackle Ghana's power gap?"

His reply: "If you can solve our power problem, you will become a hero." At the time, Kofi was living twelve hours sor followed by twelve hours dum.

Soon after, Nicole booked a plane ticket to Accra, the capital of Ghana, for a scouting mission. Kofi set up meetings for her with government officials and villagers.

It did not take Nicole long to understand the constant stress of life with unreliable power. Kofi's flashlight lived permanently in his hand. He carted power cords everywhere he went, one for each device, so he could charge whenever there was light, wherever he might be. "You are always making sure [your devices] are 100 percent charged up because you don't know if you are going to have power the next hour, or how many hours it will be down," Nicole came to see. But that was actually the least of it. In many areas beyond the capital, there was no power in homes at all. Just to charge a phone, many villagers had to walk into town and then pay to charge the phone.

The blackouts and no-power zones in many African countries have multiple causes. Government-run power utilities often do not have adequate funds to build power infrastructure out to remote areas. There has also been increased drought due to climate change, which causes problems. Much electricity in Ghana is hydroelectric, meaning produced by rivers. Low water from droughts means low power production.

Power outages are not just a drag. They are hurting the environment. When the lights blink off, locals pull out their diesel backup generators. These spew nasty pollution. Where there is no electric grid at all, cooking and home heating happens with fire. People burn firewood, coal, crop waste, and kerosene. These fuels are a major source of black carbon, the second-biggest driver of climate change after CO_2. And when forests are coming down to feed those home fires, it means CO_2 is no longer sequestered in the trees; it means global warming increases.

After her visit, Nicole revealed her problem-solving idea to investors: she was going to launch a power company comprised of tiny, localized solar-powered generators. Each generator would be part of a "mini-grid" or solar garden, which would hold the power generated by the sun and then disperse it to local homes as any utility would. She would be building entire regions' electric grids from the ground up. Bonus: the electricity would be from 100 percent renewable energy, produce zero emissions, and have minimal infrastructure costs.

Once the plan came together, she brought it directly to the people it would affect most. To one villager, Nicole promised that her solar mini-grids would be "like McDonald's"—always reliable, always the same. The villager blurted, "What's McDonald's?" Nicole laughed. Apparently, the Big Mac had not reached this town. But the villager understood everything else. And he took it seriously. He said, "Can you come back tomorrow?"

She did. Her company, Energicity, installed its first micro solar power "plant" in Ghana in October 2015, just eight months after her initial visit.

With each mini-grid added, local life improves dramatically. Kofihui-krom, one of the first Ghanian towns Energicity served, received twenty-two solar panels. Now the local clinic no longer had to deliver babies by candlelight. The local fish seller, who several times a week was riding six miles by motorbike and then another nine miles by minibus to buy her fish—and then back again to sell it before it rotted—now stores her fish in a plug-in freezer, which means nothing goes bad; her inventory lasts longer, meaning fewer daylong buying trips are required; and she earns five times what she used to. Another street vendor, now able to offer cold drinks, has seen her daily wage go from one dollar to eleven dollars—a 1,000 percent increase.

Over time, Energicity began expanding beyond Ghana, in part because the government of Ghana was acting prickly about renewing her licensing, declaring that only the national utility could sell electricity. Luckily, she had already been launching mini-grid projects in Sierra Leone and Benin. By the end of 2021, she was providing clean power to 75,000 people. Her plan was to focus on continued expansion in Sierra Leone and Benin, and to enter Liberia, where she had already received a grant to cover Energicity's launch there, in 2022. She is gunning to power a million households by 2026.

Now, you don't launch a company like Energicity if you have doubts about your ability to do something that's never been done before, on a scale that staggers the imagination.

It helps that Nicole was taught to believe in herself—from birth. Growing up in Houston, Texas, education was everything in her family. Her mom was the first Black woman to earn a master's degree in history at Vanderbilt University. Her dad, once denied admission to Baylor University because of the color of his skin, is now their first Black tenured professor. Nicole was the first Black student at her prestigious elementary school. Photographed alongside nineteen white children in her yearbook, Nicole told her parents she "just didn't notice" she looked different.

But as she grew up, she noticed she was different in another way—"nerdy." She often found herself on the outside of social cliques in middle school and high school, which just caused her to further bury her nose in books. One year, her summer reading assignment was to finish one book; Nicole read fifty. Some of her faves: *Harriet the Spy, A Wrinkle in Time,* "anything with a dragon."

All that studiousness paid off. She graduated from Yale in three quick years. She didn't love the place, so was eager to move on. "It was mean girls on steroids," she recalled. Her early career choices were safe and conventional. She joined investment bank J.P. Morgan. She reasoned, "If I wanted to have any power in the world, I needed to understand banking and money." She also had school loans to pay. Her outlet for her wilder side during this phase was New York City's all-night club scene. She would party until four a.m., then head directly back to work and "fall asleep under my desk for two hours."

Then came Harvard Business School and a job with New York mayor Michael Bloomberg's economic development team. All this early financial and business training gave her the guts to ultimately chase after Energicity. (Her go-to tip to young women coming up: "Learn to love something . . . but get the skills first.")

"Learn to love something . . . but get the skills first."

Of course, she's had her share of frustrating setbacks, dealing with Africa's bureaucracy high among them. A single banking transaction routinely takes Nicole forty-five minutes. The Ghanaian government is basically booting her out. Roads are so rutted there that her trips into villages often start in trucks and end on foot. After investing in creating an Energicity smartphone app to help users chart electric use and expenses, she discovered that most villagers owned only basic flip phones.

"Electricity is a human right."

Activism keeps her pushing forward. "Electricity is a human right." Africa's ability to develop into a society with greater opportunity for all hinges on powering every last square mile. Electricity from a renewable resource will dramatically cut disease, death, poverty, pollution, and most any other scourge you can think up. It is used to purify water, cool vaccines, warm preemie babies, allow late-night studying, get girls into schools, and spread joy. Nicole recently returned to a small village she helped electrify. She was greeted by a five-foot stereo speaker blasting music, and a huge dance party. "They had never been able to do that before."

Tara Houska

Tribal Attorney, Activist, and Founder of

the Giniw Collective

Leading the next Standing Rock

I AM ODDLY GOOD AT: singing

I AM ODDLY BAD AT: scheduling

MY GREATEST FEAR: not being as effective as I can be

THE TRAIT I MOST DEPLORE IN MYSELF: procrastination

AN OCCASION WHEN I LIE: If I don't recognize someone and they recognize me. I'll dance around it.

A WORD OR PHRASE I MOST OVERUSE: "actually"

A HABIT I'M TRYING TO GIVE UP: inability to delegate

SOMETHING I USED TO DO BEFORE I REALIZED HOW BAD IT WAS FOR THE ENVIRONMENT: purchase ready-to-wear Target cheap clothes—things made by stolen labor

A group of thirty sweaty teenage runners changed Tara Houska's life. The date was August 5, 2016, and Tara had been anxiously awaiting the youths' arrival. She had been closely following the news coverage of their progress moving through the midwestern states heading southeast, and now they were finally arriving triumphantly in Washington, DC, their final destination. The teens, many of them Native Americans like her, were staging a protest. They had run from the Standing Rock Sioux Tribe reservation in North Dakota some two thousand miles to the US Army Corps of Engineers headquarters near the Capitol. They had a message for the US government: stop sending oil through the thousand-mile Dakota pipeline. And get off our sacred lands!

As a member of the Bear Clan from Couchiching First Nation and an indigenous rights attorney and activist, Tara had been fighting the same fight in DC for three years. Most recently, she had been acting as Advisor, Native American Affairs, for Bernie Sanders's campaign. But somehow the teens' actions felt bigger than anything she'd achieved through official legal action or legislation. "I'd seen a lot of resistance actions, but this felt different."

Somehow the teens' actions felt bigger than anything she'd achieved through official legal action or legislation.

She was moved to follow their lead. Within a month, she was in a rental car heading to Standing Rock. For the next six months, she protested alongside hundreds—and eventually thousands—of other environmentalists who camped beside the Cannonball River, physically blocking pipeline construction. Through the subzero winter, they held prayer circles, lit ceremonial fires, chained themselves to bulldozers, and shared smoked salmon gifted by Northwest tribes.

Walking away from her life in DC felt like the most reasonable thing to do. The Dakota pipeline threatened everything she believed in.

The Dakota pipeline threatened everything she believed in.

At Standing Rock, Tara held up her car mat to ward off police officers' rubber bullets. She advocated on behalf of the over seven hundred arrested protesters. She was arrested herself and put into a dog kennel. She responded to being treated like a dog with plenty of loud howling.

While no neat victory was achieved, and the oil has been flowing since May 2017, much was gained. In 2020, a US district court judge ordered a more extensive environmental review as demanded by the Standing Rock Sioux Tribe, and a key permit was yanked. One court ordered the pipeline shut during the review, but the shutdown was appealed, so oil flow continues for now. Tara, along with a delegation of Indigenous women, pressured banks to withhold billions in loans they were slated to provide to finance the Dakota Access Pipeline. Native people stood their ground, capturing the world's attention and support. Police brutality against Native Americans made international news and helped demonize the oil company's violation of treaties. North Dakota Governor Doug Burgum assured North Dakota Native Americans that he would "include them" in all environmental discussions affecting the state. And a loud chorus that includes Hollywood heavyweights has called for President Biden to shut the pipeline down. Tara's personal takeaway: "Direct action is one of the most effective forms of advocacy." Even though "it requires some discomfort."

Tara never returned to DC after her six-month stint at Standing Rock.

She gave up her law practice and most of her consulting gigs with Indigenous-rights groups. And she moved back to Minnesota, where she'd been raised, and built a makeshift pipeline resistance camp in the woods, where she has lived without electricity or running water since 2018. She calls her grassroots, women-led effort Giniw Collective, after the Ojibwe word for "the golden eagle." Her frontline camp is strategically located on the banks of the Mississippi River near Palisade, Minnesota, two hundred yards from the trench that Canadian oil giant Enbridge dug for their Line 3 pipeline project.

That's right. Tara is taking on another massive pipeline now. To her, every mile of steel tube slated to carry toxic material through her home represents the same fight: Native Americans vs. Big Oil.

Every mile of steel tube slated to carry toxic material through her home represents the same fight: Native Americans vs. Big Oil.

Starting in late 2021, the Line 3 pipeline is scheduled to carry nine hundred thousand gallons of tar sands oil every day—the most climate-damaging form of oil—from Alberta, Canada, to Lake Huron. According to many experts, there is nowhere worse on earth to lay this pipe. The Great Lakes provide 85 percent of America's fresh water.

Enbridge has a terrible track record with spills and contamination. They are best known for spewing 840,000 barrels of oil into the Kalamazoo River in Michigan, plus over a thousand other spills throughout North America. Add to this the fact that the yearly emissions from this single pipeline will be equivalent to fifty coal power plants—greater than all current emissions in Minnesota combined, which will wipe out all gains the state plans to make to address climate change.

The pipeline also crosses eight hundred wetlands, many on reservations very near Tara's Minnesota homeland, which have sustained her people and hold spiritual and practical significance. "My ancestors were told by the creator to search for a home where the food floats on water. This is the only place where that happens." Native Americans still harvest the wild rice "like we have for thousands of years," using cedar knockers to hit the rice into their canoes.

At Tara's camp, a group gathers daily at ten a.m. for a prayer circle. They pray for the water. The rice. The planet. The animals and fish. "The circle grows larger every day," she adds.

Tara did not always stand up for her Native lands or her identity. Growing up in a small town, only one of a handful of Native American children at her school, she was made to feel less-than. It was an inheritance. For centuries, her people were made to feel less-than. Her own grandmother was one of thousands of Native Americans forced into boarding schools to have their cultural heritage drilled out of them. And so when it was Tara's turn to assimilate, she "made Native jokes" at her own expense. "That's how I dealt with the shame." Growing up in a mixed-race household, she felt her difference acutely. She wanted any identity "that wasn't the one I had." The result was that she went through some extreme teenage phases—"goth, punk, you name it."

And then she came back to her Native self.

Now that deep connection to the land, fostered by her Native roots, drives everything. Now she appreciates that she grew up hunting, fishing, eating deer, and berry picking. "Natives have a sane relationship to land because we understand we are dependent on it," she explains. The oil companies scare her because they share none of that sense of dependence.

As with the Dakota pipeline, she is fighting with the political skills she acquired in Washington and the boots-on-the-ground tactics she's learned since: Go after the money. Lobby the banks—here and abroad—to defund, defund, defund the pipelines. Use the legal system to slow the process. Meet with powerful allies like Minnesota Congresswoman Ilhan Omar. Move a piano to block construction on the nearby pipeline. Or tweet @Biden, "Suspending one big oil expansion project through Native territory and approving another is the opposite of climate leadership. You stopped KXL #nowdoline3." About the last, she is waiting for his response.

FACT: Alberta's tar sands oil—which Enbridge Line 3 pipeline transports—is among the dirtiest and most carbon-intensive fuel sources on the planet, emitting 14 to 20 percent more planet-warming gases than the conventional oil that is typically found in US refineries.

VI

The Techno-Vators

Lisa Dyson

Cofounder and Chief Executive Officer of

Air Protein

and Cofounder and Chair of

Kiverdi, Inc.

Making meat (and more) from thin air

I AM ODDLY GOOD AT: finding things

I AM ODDLY BAD AT: giving up

MY GREATEST FEAR: having a lack of options

THE TRAIT I MOST DEPLORE IN MYSELF: I'm okay with myself.

AN OCCASION WHEN I LIE: When someone cooks for me, their food is good, no matter what my taste buds have to say about it. :)

A WORD OR PHRASE I MOST OVERUSE: "It sounds like . . ." I've learned that it's good to play back to people what I heard them say, to communicate that I'm listening and to ensure that my understanding is correct.

SOMETHING I USED TO DO BEFORE I REALIZED HOW BAD IT WAS FOR THE ENVIRONMENT: cavalier about plastic bag use

NASA had a problem in 1960, back when it was planning its first trip to Mars. Engineers needed to identify or create a food that could be packed into a cramped rocket capsule and that would sustain a crew for a year or several. A team of scientists began researching the problem. They made real progress. But that rocket to Mars never took off—money and ambition went out of the American space program—and the super-food that would have fed those space travelers was never made.

The essence of the Mars rocket meal plan was this: Plants suck carbon dioxide from the air into their leaves, and with the sun's energy, plus water, convert everything to sugars—their food. Astronauts hurtling through space at twenty-five thousand mph exhale carbon dioxide 24/7. In other words, the gas in those out breaths was plant food. The rocket could sustain plant life, but that would take too much space and time to grow. But there are microbes, tiny living organisms too small to be seen by the naked eye, called hydrogenotrophs, that feed on carbon dioxide, too. With hydrogen (from water) added, these microbes turn into "supercharged carbon recyclers" that transform carbon dioxide into cellular material quickly, and in a very small space. Edible cellular material.

It was an astonishing discovery, but save a few published scientific papers, NASA's quirky finding faded into obscurity. Until physicist Lisa Dyson and her colleague from grad school John Reed dug it up in 2008, turning the out-there astronaut sustenance concept into something far more practical and hopefully someday quite commonplace.

First, though, Dyson had to come face to face with a hurricane—Katrina, the one that decimated New Orleans, where she had gone to live to help rebuild the city. Entire neighborhoods were washed out, turned into nothing but ghosts. There were so many refugees. Witnessing that human devastation up close, she couldn't help but feel a sense of impending doom. New Orleans's fate could be all of our fates, she thought. Life-extinguishing natural atrocities like bomb cyclones are a new norm in the age of global warming. One day, walking by a mess of bricks and ruined books, once an elementary school, she whispered to herself, "My life will be spent fighting climate change."

She knew that CO_2 is a primary driver of global warming and decided to start there. After she roped in her friend John, a fellow MIT PhD alum, they started brainstorming. Recycling carbon dioxide intrigued them. Could the abundant gas heating the atmosphere somehow be turned into useful products? Long past midnight every evening, in the glare of her computer screen, she scrolled through scientific publications. John did the same. They shared notes. This is how they found NASA's CO_2 food research. And things got very clear, very fast.

In many ways, her childhood had prepared her for this moment. The impetus for the technology had been to make astronaut travel efficient. To cut weight. This notion had a special pull for Lisa. A child of divorced parents, she was constantly moving, as her parents chased jobs, love, career dreams. She'd had eleven different homes and attended fourteen different schools before she left for college. During the last move, she refused to switch schools, waking at four a.m. instead, to make the two-hour bus commute from her new house back to finish high school in Wilmington, California.

Some of her schools were good, but the worst of them may have served her best. They forced her to become "a squeaky wheel," pushing to get her needs met. This was how she learned to code, despite attending a high

Lisa Dyson

school that offered no computing. She told her math teacher she was desperate to learn, and he then devoted his lunch hour for months in order to teach her. She knew where she needed to get.

She had a beloved cousin who'd pursued STEM, and learning about her work got Lisa hooked, too. She would pore over her cousin's painstakingly crafted structural drawings for college engineering courses and hear about her cousin's job at Hughes Aircraft. Even while her role model pushed Lisa toward engineering, she fell for physics. "For me, this was the way to understand magnetism or electricity, how math applies in the real world."

She graduated from Brandeis, and immediately applied for a Fulbright scholarship. Earning this honor took her to England for her master's program in physics at the University of London. A doctoral program at MIT came next. In 2004, Lisa became only the fourth Black woman ever to earn a PhD in theoretical high-energy physics. Her thesis connected string theory, naked singularities, black holes, and time travel. There are not a lot of people on planet Earth who can even unpack the previous sentence. Further training at Stanford and UC Berkeley followed.

But there was another layer to Lisa, hiding in plain sight, one she'd inherited from her dad, who was the president of a chain of fifty-five hair salons throughout the US. He was a consummate entrepreneur, five ideas a minute—for products, trainings, beauty schools. That business spirit was alive in Lisa as well.

Which brings us back to the Mars meal plan from NASA. Though she was a physicist, Lisa loved the biochemical magic of the CO_2 transformed into food technology, the simplicity. She knew that reactions are frequently harnessed to make one substance from another. Wine, sauerkraut, cheese, yogurt, and beer—all of these are the result of biochemistry, with bacteria and other microorganisms consuming sugars and making a new substance.

"But why stop at food?" she thought. "And why stop with sugars? What might be produced from carbon dioxide?" She and her lab partner did more research. They tracked down experts. They determined that the same processes could turn carbon dioxide into fuels of various kinds, which led to the development of a plan to slowly elbow out environmentally bad fuels.

Kiverdi, Inc., the name of their new enterprise, quickly developed a line of technical solutions. They made soil with CO_2-rich nutrients that increased crop yield and made crops resilient against droughts and other high-stress conditions. But their biggest contribution to sustainability is their palm oil alternative. Used in everything from shampoo and cosmetics to pastries and pharmaceuticals, palm oil demand is bottomless, and desperate farmers are more than happy to torch rain forests to plant more palm trees. That's a mega problem, as rain forests are our most efficient carbon absorbers. A cheap substitute for palm oil has the United Nations, the World Economic Forum, the California Energy Commission, and even the television series NOVA seriously salivating.

Then Lisa got more ambitious—with plans to feed the world. She understands that there is consensus that the world needs to increase food production by 70 percent for the projected nine billion mouths expected by 2050. So she grabbed a bunch of her teammates and launched a second company, Air Protein, to attack the problem. Their mandate: to grow meat from thin air, just as the NASA team had envisioned back in 1966. Instead of a rocket ship, the CO_2-hungry microorganisms will live inside a giant fermenter in a lab in Menlo Park and be fed a secret blend of nutrients. The output, which looks a bit like flour, is a complete protein. Rather than having to wait months (for soy) or years (for cows) for protein that's ready to eat, these proteins are ready to eat in days.

> *Their mandate: to grow meat*
> *from thin air, just as the NASA team*
> *had envisioned back in 1966.*

Best of all, the stuff is tasteless. Odd to celebrate that in a food, but here's why: it can be made to taste like anything. Add pressure and heat, and the protein can feel just like meat. Flavorings and spices could have it mistaken for a McNugget or a bacon strip. In 2019, Air Protein released chicken as its first product. Now Lisa and company are scaling up the technology so their meats can be widely available to consumers. Stay tuned on that. Analysts predict that plant-based protein and meat alternatives will be a mainstay before long, with the market ballooning to $85 billion by 2030.

> *Flavorings and spices could have it*
> *mistaken for a McNugget or a bacon strip.*

This work has led Lisa to perceive Earth as humans' spaceship. We only have one craft. We only have so much space, so many resources, and they have to last the duration of humanity's whole mission. We can't keep multiplying and multiplying and expect to have infinite resources to feed us, quench our thirst, heat our homes, power our work. We need to recycle waste into new products. That is our new hope.

FACT: Our food—the farming, production, transport, packaging, retail, and waste management processes it requires—accounts for one-third of all global greenhouse emissions, according to a 2021 report in *Nature Food*.

Lisa Jackson

*Vice President of Environment,
Policy, and Social Initiatives at*

Apple Inc.

and Former Head of

the EPA

Apple of the green movement's eye

I AM ODDLY GOOD AT: singing

I AM ODDLY BAD AT: Baking. I should be better because it's chemistry.

A GUILTY PLEASURE: watching *The Real Housewives of Atlanta*

THE TRAIT I MOST DEPLORE IN MYSELF: too little patience

AN OCCASION WHEN I LIE: to protect people's feelings

A WORD OR PHRASE I MOST OVERUSE: "what the hell"

A HABIT I'M TRYING TO GIVE UP: not exercising

SOMETHING I USED TO DO BEFORE I REALIZED HOW BAD IT WAS FOR THE ENVIRONMENT: Fire pits. I love them. But now when I see them, I see greenhouse gases.

Lisa Jackson wanted to be a mail carrier like her dad when she grew up, not the moral compass of Apple Inc. She saw how serious her father took his work, hand-distributing urgently needed Social Security checks, ferrying packages until dark on Christmas Eve. It filled her with deep respect for careers in public service. So much so that when he took her to visit his mail sorting facility, she peered up at him with her big six-year-old eyes and said, "I'm going to work here one day." To which he shot back, "No, sweetheart." He'd make sure she had more options than he'd had, as a Black man just home from World War II, living in New Orleans. He promised her, there are all kinds of ways to serve.

In fact, he had big plans for Lisa's future, a future he'd been imagining since he'd first seen her at a Catholic orphanage in 1962. She'd been just two weeks old. Three years later, on a trip to DC, he had her pose for a photo in her frilly white dress in front of the White House. "Look here, sweetheart," he said, pointing to the grand mansion. "You're going to work there someday."

He would not live to see how right he was. In 2009, Lisa was posing for photos with President Obama in the Oval Office. The new president had just appointed her to head the Environmental Protection Agency. That afternoon, she walked her mom around the grand dark-wood-paneled office where she would oversee seventeen thousand employees and a budget of $8 billion. By coincidence, the location was the original headquarters of the postmaster general of the United States, and every day, her stiletto ankle boots clicked across the great postal seal embedded in the marble floor, reminding her of her dad and her duty.

Lisa's appointment as head administrator of the EPA was preceded by twenty-five years in government environmental protection jobs: sixteen years in New York's region two EPA office, focused on hazardous waste, Superfund sites, and industrial pollution; and nine years in New Jersey's

Department of Environmental Protection as assistant commissioner of compliance and enforcement, and eventually as commissioner.

Her best career advice for young people: "Learn your trade." She could make federal policy impacting communities because she had been in those communities, learning firsthand what they were facing.

One could argue that her career began in grade school with an HP programmable calculator. It was 1978, and the school year was wrapping up, when she learned Tulane University would be hosting an academic summer program for high school juniors. The HP calculator was the draw—every participant got one. She applied and got in. The program would be her first exposure to engineering, a career that would lead her to the White House.

It was also around this time that news of the Hooker Chemical Company filled the airwaves, specifically the dumping of twenty-one thousand tons of chemicals, including known carcinogens, into Love Canal, which ran alongside eight hundred homes outside Niagara Falls, New York. She thought: "If chemical engineers made those nasty toxins exploding up through backyards, chemical engineers are best suited to find the solution to clean them up." She decided to be one of those chemical engineers. After graduating from high school as valedictorian, she returned to Tulane for college, ironically on a scholarship offered by Shell Oil. She even spent a summer working for them doing gas plant maintenance in a hard hat and iron-toed shoes. She then continued to Princeton University for her master's in chemical engineering.

But even twenty-five years of training could not have prepared Lisa for the catastrophe she faced fifteen months into her tenure as head of the EPA. On the night of April 20, 2010, a concrete cap just installed to close an offshore oil well off from further use came unsealed. Flammable natural gas escaped from the underground well, surging up onto BP's drilling rig Deepwater Horizon, igniting into a ball of fire and eventually sinking the whole rig. Eleven workers were killed. "As the picture came into view, it was not a good one," Lisa said, recalling the first briefing on the incident. Before all was done, over 130 million gallons of oil was released from that well into the Gulf of Mexico. The spill remains the largest man-made environmental disaster in human history.

Lisa had to make quick decisions about how to stem the damage, including weighing the trade-offs and ultimately approving BP's use of massive quantities of a nasty chemical "dispersant" to break up the oil before surface slicks destroyed wetlands and all that lived there. An added kick in Lisa's gut was that the destruction of habitats and livelihoods occurred in her own backyard, the region all around her beloved hometown of New Orleans.

Tangling with Congress was another reality of her time at the EPA, as is typical for the role, given the fundamental standoff between industry and environmental concerns. In the midterm elections in 2010, Republicans gained control of the House, which emboldened anti-regulation corporations and the congresspeople protecting them, and she became one of their favorite punching bags. At one point, while fighting power plants and the "tons and tons" of mercury they were emitting, she was accused of killing jobs and "putting the American economy in a straightjacket." She held her own. One Texas Republican, funded mostly by oil and gas companies, mocked her "tons and tons of mercury" attack, "given that power plants record amounts in pounds per year, not tons," he said. She came right back: "Per plant, yes sir, but if you aggregate them and add them up, you get pounds, and two thousand pounds equals a ton."

> *In 2010, Republicans gained control of the House,*
> *which emboldened anti-regulation corporations and the*
> *congresspeople protecting them, and she became one of their*
> *favorite punching bags.*

Despite these political fights, Lisa managed historic victories. A momentous first was getting greenhouse gases characterized as pollutants under the Clean Air Act. This savvy move allowed the EPA to negotiate strict new emissions standards for cars, marking the first government action to limit pollutants that cause global warming. That's big. Her car standards did away with billions of tons of carbon dioxide emissions and brought a doubling of fuel efficiency in the transportation fleet. With Obama's first term coming to a close, Lisa started contemplating where else she might contribute to the environmental fight.

This time, she jumped as far from the government game as possible, to the heart of Silicon Valley, land of independent thinking and freewheeling innovators. She had met now CEO of Apple Tim Cook when he came to one of the gatherings of business leaders she pulled together at the EPA. The two clicked and eventually started talking about how she might help Apple Computer supercharge their environmental efforts. What attracted Lisa to a computer company, the epitome of runaway consumerism, a place known for changing the jack size for plugs and earphones to force constant replacement and creating snazzier models at lightning speed to create constant upgrade fever? She believes that only people who are crazy enough to think they can change the world will do it—and that Apple is that kind of crazy. This company, which in mid-2020 had the most profitable quarter of any company ever, was blowing up every norm, turning your phone into a computer and then into a wristwatch; remaking

Hollywood and the music industry. As the world's most valuable company, they hold unfathomable market sway and cultural power.

Her intent was to take the company to the forefront of environmental reform "using everything Apple has and is" to start ripples that could move outward across all industries. "This is not very Apple, but we encouraged people to copy us," she said. Her boldest move yet is a pledge to achieve carbon neutrality by 2030 across all the company's operations, suppliers, and customers. This means that the maker of your AirPods, the snazzy box they come in, the transport to get them to the Apple store or your home, and the energy to charge them, have net-zero impact. The goal? As far as the environment, the earth, and global warming are concerned, it will be as though Apple doesn't exist.

The goal? As far as the environment, the earth, and global warming are concerned, it will be as though Apple doesn't exist.

Under Lisa, Apple is on track to rid their packaging of all plastic by 2025, with moves like using paperboard to hold AirPods, or adding cuts and folds to hold products in place. Less plastic packaging means more paper use, which they offset with investment in sustainable forests. Apple is rejecting conventional clear-cutting, which destroys all the trees that helpfully pull carbon dioxide from the air, and instead is supporting logging practices that keep forests intact. With Conservation International, Apple is maintaining mangrove forests in Colombia, South America—forests that are uniquely effective at storing carbon. This single project reduces CO_2

emissions enough to offset the emissions that result from running the vehicle fleet they use to update Apple Maps.

A favorite recycling advance under Lisa is Daisy and Dave, robots that disassemble phones and computers for their component parts. Daisy can tear through two hundred devices per hour.

Converting to clean power is another star on Lisa's achievements slate. In 2018, Apple launched a $300 million fund to invest in developing clean energy sources in China. Apple has built two of the world's largest onshore wind turbines in Denmark and a solar farm in Nevada to power data sites.

The highest but most important hurdle is "working outside of Apple, to push transformation among suppliers," Lisa said. The strategy is to lead by example. In 2016, Apple achieved 100 percent clean energy use in their retail stores, data centers, and corporate offices. Through trainings and technical assistance, 110 of their suppliers are on track to reach net-zero carbon output by 2030.

Yet, through all this business reform, Lisa's gaze remains most piercingly on bettering communities. "Some people in the environmental space are motivated by preserving natural beauty. That's not me. I am motivated by people. Every one of these things impacts communities. I don't care whether it's ten people who are impacted or ten thousand. To each one, that is their life and community," she said.

> **FACT:** Manufacturing one new iPhone uses as much energy as recharging and operating a smartphone for an entire decade, *Fast Company* reported. The vast majority of the energy expenditure comes from mining the rare minerals inside.

FACT: Running your devices, doing Google searches, and posting to your Instagram Story all use serious energy. A single Instagram post from soccer star Cristiano Ronaldo to his 240 million followers consumes as much energy as ten United Kingdom households, a 2020 investigation into the environmental impact of social media revealed. Ariana Grande, with nearly as many followers, same story.

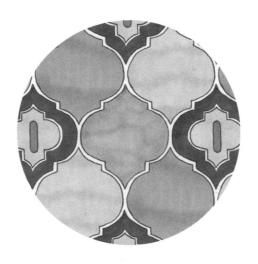

Daniela Fernandez

Founder and Chief Executive Officer of

Sustainable Ocean Alliance

Spurring the next Industrial Revolution—for oceans

I AM ODDLY GOOD AT: reading people

I AM ODDLY BAD AT: reading maps

MY GREATEST FEAR: losing my intellectual ability with old age

THE TRAIT I MOST DEPLORE IN MYSELF: impatience

AN OCCASION WHEN I LIE: to tell someone they look good in their clothes

A WORD OR PHRASE I MOST OVERUSE: "urgency"

SOMETHING I USED TO DO BEFORE I REALIZED HOW BAD IT WAS FOR THE ENVIRONMENT: Lights on everywhere all the time. I love light.

In 2014, during her freshman year at Georgetown, Daniela Fernandez was invited to a climate conference at the United Nations. She caught the train to New York City, passed through the UN's tight security, and spent the day in awe. The sponsor that sent her—the Georgetown Scholarship Program that had granted her a full ride to college—had failed to mention that she would be seated among world leaders and business moguls. Seated to her left, Palau's ambassador to the United Nations; to her right, Italy's representative; behind her, a top Google exec.

The topic that day was the state of the oceans, which, despite her focus on environmental issues, Daniela knew very little about. The talks were one endless wave of bad news: acidification, dwindling biodiversity, decomposing coral, marine dead zones, fish die-offs, inadequate carbon storage. Covering 71 percent of the earth, and responsible for capturing and storing 40 percent of the carbon that humans release into the atmosphere, the oceans could not be more critical to planetary survival. At day's end, as she was heading to the cocktail reception, it hit Daniela that no one had spoken of solutions.

The next night, back in her dorm room, she scribbled "Sustainable Ocean Alliance (SOA)" across the top of a notepad. And just like that, it was launched, a new youth-led crusade focused entirely on oceans. The plan? She'd fire up an army of young ocean protectors, creating "hubs" where they could learn, advocate, organize, and build solutions. She'd teach leadership, share science, anoint speakers. And she'd tap the leaders she'd met at the UN and secure their blessing. (Wisely, she'd come home with a purse side pocket's worth of business cards.)

Her first major action was a conference on campus. She boldly invited Secretary of State John Kerry (he became Biden's climate czar in 2021) and legendary marine biologist Sylvia Earle. Students came from all over the country, then returned to their campuses and launched SOA chapters. At her own chapter, Daniela pressed Georgetown to offer its first-ever course on oceans and the environment. She wanted to take that class, "so I had to create one," she said. She recruited environmental policy heavyweight Monica Medina to teach the course (Medina became Biden's nominee for

Assistant Secretary of State for Oceans and International Environmental and Science affairs).

Over time, more and more SOA members started coming to her with ideas for ocean rehab technologies—for example, a method to fortify coral, and a means of harnessing wave power. "If I just had some funding and guidance, I would give my idea a go," they'd say. This gave Daniela a new inspiration. "In the Industrial Revolution, we had all these inventors and scientific discoveries. It was a constant pipeline of trial and error, trial and error. [The ideas] didn't all work, but that's how you get to the ones that do work. Lots and lots of tries." So, Daniela started plotting SOA 2.0, a program that helped tiny companies experiment with and pay for ocean-fixing solutions.

As graduation neared, Daniela faced a crossroads: Should she move SOA to Silicon Valley and risk living the unstable life of a fledgling entrepreneur, or should she accept one of several high-paying job offers from Wall Street banks? She consulted family and friends. Those who knew her backstory—immigrant from Ecuador, raised by a single mom whose wages came from IHOP and newspaper delivery—urged her to choose the safe route.

Daniela didn't listen. Despite having zero funding for SOA or any real financial safety net for herself, she chose risk and independence. "I took the approach of Hernán Cortés in Spain," she said. "Burn all the ships so you can't turn back."

"I took the approach of Hernán Cortés in Spain," she said. "Burn all the ships so you can't turn back."

Burning her ships is actually a habit. As a teenager in Chicago, she pledged to convert her high school to solar. Then she came up with a plan to make it happen: she put on a big and lucrative school talent show. "The panels are still there today," she proudly notes. Then, right after Georgetown, while still in SOA 1.0, the European Union invited her to co-host an ocean conference in Malta. Daniela accepted on the spot and agreed to turn out two hundred youth leaders and entrepreneurs . . . two hundred youth leaders and entrepreneurs she hadn't identified or met, yet. Then, in Malta, having secured the two hundred attendees, she committed to bringing a hundred more to the Our Ocean Conference hosted by the Indonesian government the following summer, AND she promised to help launch a hundred ocean-saving companies, at the same time. She attributes this speak-first-solve-later streak to her upbringing. There were always rough situations, and she was always finding a way through.

She's been blessed by great timing. On the eve of her Silicon Valley move, all the funding for SOA's "accelerator" offshoot and her own living expenses . . . were still TBD. Adding stress, her mom had just lost a new job as a live-in caretaker, which meant she had nowhere to sleep. She needed Daniela's help. Things looked grim, and Daniela decided she had to reverse her big decision. Later that week, her SOA fundraising meeting with a bank executive turned into a job interview. "I know I'm here to pitch you on SOA, but do you think Wells Fargo might need someone like me?" she asked, suddenly desperate to have a salaried job and stabilize her family. The savvy banker went a different way. He dangled a $10,000 check and said she could have it if she could convince five other funders to match his SOA gift. She got her $60,000.

She lived on that money for months, but eventually her account ran dry and panic set in again. Even worse, she now had a business partner, Craig Dudenhoeffer, who trusted her to keep SOA afloat. Racking her brain for fundraising ideas, she remembered a tip she'd heard about a donor who backed social enterprises and was called "Pine" but kept his real identity anonymous. He had a website set up for receiving proposals, but she skipped the formal application and, near midnight, emailed him using a general-info address she found on the site. At five a.m. the next day, someone named Pine emailed back, offering SOA a million dollars. "I still have no idea who 'Pine' is," she said, laughing. "I send him updates, and he responds. I had to convert the million from Bitcoin." More great timing.

Daniela's superpower is a willingness to ask for help. She has lured in Salesforce CEO Marc Benioff, who then touted Daniela and SOA onstage at the World Economic Forum in Davos, the kind of exposure nonprofit and business founders die for. The next year, at a nonprofit gala, she approached Sven Lindblad, the owner of a high-end adventure-cruise business, for help. She started by telling him about the five start-ups she'd helped launch, including one making straws from seaweed that dissolve in a few hours. Then she turned things around and asked, "What is the legacy you want to leave behind in the world?" He confessed he wanted to use boats to educate youths. "Well, you have boats, and I have youths," she shot back. The next thing she knew, she was flying to New York to pitch to his team an idea for a floating summit that would include rich financiers, ocean experts, and the eco-entrepreneurs SOA was helping launch. Sven was all in. There was such good juju when that "Accelerator at Sea," as Daniela named it, quickly came to pass that several billionaires on board opened their wallets.

By this time, 2019, Daniela was in major expansion mode, and the infusion of cash was essential. She was offering mentoring and $25,000 to fifteen new start-ups, including one that made a Styrofoam substitute from discarded shrimp shells, and another that tracked unregulated fishing and prevented accidental "bycatch" of sea turtles and fish.

We must get the oceans back in order—fast. Daniela is growing her army. In 2020, Daniela supported nine more start-ups working to save our oceans. She is on track to bring another twenty-five ventures under SOA's wing by the end of 2022. She continues to recruit young people who have grassroots ocean projects, and companies with novel and compelling ideas. She issues a rallying cry for the next generation to fight to save our ocean and planet—and prevail.

FACT: Sea turtles may become extinct because increasingly the babies are all—or nearly all—female. Ocean warming—that's why. The temperature of the sand that female sea turtles nest in influences the gender of their offspring. The lower, cooler eggs become males during incubation, while the warmer top eggs become females, and the conditions that provide cooler sand are disappearing.

Hot Idea? Meet Your Support Squad.

Incubators and accelerators are start-up "support" programs that have proliferated as fast as flavored fizzy water brands in recent years. The idea is to help a business or nonprofit get launched with mentors, business connections, resources, lab/office space, and usually some funding. About one-third of the green ventures included in this book benefited from one or more such programs. Here are a few to check out:

Elemental Excelerator: Annually funding fifteen to twenty companies and nonprofits focusing on sustainable water management, agriculture, energy usage, waste, and transportation. Ventures can apply to access up to a million dollars in funding. www.elemental -excelerator.com

Sustainable Ocean Alliance: Daniela Fernandez at SOA runs Ocean Solutions Accelerator, the first of its kind, focused specifically on addressing our most critical ocean challenges. Participants do four weeks of immersive content, mentorship, and relationship-building. www.soalliance.org

Echoing Green Fellowship: A world-renowned, two-year program for social entrepreneurs. Climate is a priority area, and participants receive seed funding and extensive support. www.echoinggreen.org

Y Combinator: The behemoth of start-up incubators, YC has backed notables Airbnb and Dropbox. They are currently reaching out to attract ventures in carbon removal, clean transportation, clean meat, cheap energy, and energy storage and transmission. They run four cohorts yearly. www.ycombinator.com

Imagine H$_2$O: Focused on the water sector, Imagine H$_2$O connects entrepreneurs with world leaders in water, government, and social enterprise to help turn ideas into solutions. Selected entrepreneurs participate in Imagine H$_2$O's annual innovation program, and winning teams continue in the business accelerator. www.imagineh2o.org

Techstars: In partnership with the Nature Conservancy, Techstars Denver supports entrepreneurs "helping people and nature thrive together." In other locales of this national organization, Techstars offers a selection of other subject-specific accelerators like Farm to Fork. www.techstars.com

Greentown Labs: A climate tech incubator where members pay monthly fees for lab or office space. Considerations for membership: climate tech and cleantech focus, business and technology stage, and community fit. Over two hundred eighty companies have incubated here. www.greentownlabs.com

IndieBio: Each start-up team receives $250,000 in seed funding, lab and co-working space, dedicated mentorship, and access to a huge network of alumni, investors, biotech entrepreneurs, press, and potential corporate partners. Early-stage biology companies move to downtown San Francisco or Manhattan to take part in an intense four-month program that runs twice a year, with fifteen companies in each program. Michelle Zhu and Tammy Hsu began Huue here. www.indiebio.co

Food System 6: A three-month program with six to eight companies focused on food and agriculture. Areas of focus include: circularity, healthy people, vibrant farms, sustainable ecosystems, and justice and fairness. www.foodsystem6.org

Jamie Bainbridge

Vice President of Product Development at

Bolt Threads

The mistress of mushroom leather

I AM ODDLY GOOD AT: parallel parking

I AM ODDLY BAD AT: computer admin

MY GREATEST FEAR: snakes

A GUILTY PLEASURE: sugar

THE TRAIT I MOST DEPLORE IN MYSELF: being judgmental

A HABIT I'M TRYING TO GIVE UP: Sugar. COVID-19 made my habit worse.

SOMETHING I USED TO DO BEFORE I REALIZED HOW BAD IT WAS FOR THE ENVIRONMENT: not think about the packaging of what I buy

Jamie Bainbridge was an upcycler long before it was trendy. In high school she scrounged bits of technical outdoor fabric to sew backpacks and parkas for friends. When one of her homemade ski coats needed stuffing to become a down puff, she slipped into her parents' bedroom, cut a teeny slit in the comforter, and extracted a handful of feathers. When the next coat was ready for fill, she returned . . . and again. "I did it enough that, of course, Mom eventually noticed," she said, laughing.

Nowadays her upcycling is less hobby and more maniacal obsession. And it's directed exclusively at leather.

Nowadays her upcycling is less hobby and more maniacal obsession.

Yes, Nike Blazers and Blundstone ankle boots may be very fashionable, but they necessitate herds upon herds of cows farting and belching out heat-trapping greenhouse gases. We know why that's a problem. But the pollution doesn't end there. Once a tannery has got a dead cow on its hands, there's this "hide covered with hair, which comes from the animal's backside, which is full of fat, and you have to take that putrefying hide and render it sterile, which means you need a hell of a lot of chemicals," Jamie detailed. You can hear in her voice that she's totally grossed out. From calf to tannery, it's an ecological quagmire. No surprise, leather is an industry under attack and in decline. "The writing is on the wall," she says.

But Jamie has no intention of asking anyone to forgo cool black boots and motorcycle jackets. Instead, she's manufacturing "clean" leather or "green" leather. Her company's replacement for cows is . . . mushrooms. Well, a part of the mushroom root, to be very exact. Yes, mushrooms are magical in many ways.

The chronology of discovery-to-fabrication went something like this: in 2015, Jamie joined Bolt Threads, a daring bio-materials start-up in Emeryville, California, as VP of product development. Back then, Bolt's focus was bioengineered silk; Bolt used microorganisms, instead of silkworms, to brew a substance that could be spun into silk thread. That was all exciting and good, but then Jamie and team stumbled across a tiny company making computer packaging from mushroom roots. This tiny company was also exploring making leather from the same fungi. Suddenly, microorganisms spinning silk seemed less thrilling to the Bolt team, compared to mushroom roots that could be turned into a convincing leather purse or pair of high tops. The root system of a mushroom is a fast-growing dense network of fibers called mycelium (the mushroom you eat on your pizza is like a flower, growing up from these roots). Jamie and team quickly inked a licensing deal that allowed Bolt to make products with the mycelium technology.

For Jamie and Bolt, mycelium tech is one of those rare, bullseye discoveries that can affect the environment in a major way, disrupting a whole industry overnight. It's what environmentalists dream of. That's because true environmental change requires clean, alternative methods, or products with lightning-speed growth potential that can replace the status quo now. And the replacement thing—in this case mushrooms—needs to be as good as what it's replacing, and—hardest part—reproducible in high quantities. Mycelium meets all the criteria. What assured Jamie? Seeing what happened when she left a "leather" sample lying around the office. "People would pick it up, and they could just not stop touching it. That's when I knew."

"People would pick it up, and they could just not stop touching it. That's when I knew."

Her journey to become the mistress of mushroom leather started in 1979. She was a newly minted forestry major at the University of Washington, working for the Burlington Northern Railroad in Washington State, a surveying job that stank from the start. Her boss's first words to her: "Damn, they sent me a girl." Jamie decided to take her frustration to her dad, who handed her a beer and challenged her to a pool match.

"Problem is, you are not doing what you are supposed to be doing," her dad counseled, as he leaned down and eyed his shot line. What she was "supposed to be doing" was heeding her passion for and talent with fabric—sewing, fabricating. Her dad always knew how to steer her right.

She quit the surveying job and was soon designing tents for Early Winters, a pioneer of outdoor fabrics and the first to make a tent from Gore-Tex. From there, she hopped around in product and textile design—at Patagonia, Banana Republic, Nike, Nau, and finally Bolt.

As her expertise grew, so did her disgust over her industry's practices. Textile production and leather tanning account for 20 percent of the earth's water pollution, as well as all that methane. "I'd seen the effluent flowing out of factories, with fibers piled up on shorelines like lint from your dryer. It was whatever color clothes were being made that day," she said. Bolt Threads spoke to her because Bolt was for total reinvention.

That brings us back to mushrooms' mycelium root system. In a way, Jamie is finally putting her forestry degree to work, because the process of making material from mushroom "roots" replicates what happens beneath the forest floors. To get these rootlike tendrils to reproduce at the scale needed, scientists bring the mushroom spores indoors and grow them on a tray holding a bed of sawdust and other organic materials that act as a substrate—or the food to fuel growth. All these trays are stacked in what looks like a shipping container. What happens is that as the spores start consuming substrate and growing, they create a layer of new growth at the top of the tray. It's almost like sheets of giant marshmallows. They feel like marshmallows, too. The foamy layer is what ultimately becomes the leather, or "Mylo," as they call it.

Then, in a process too hush-hush and top secret to even describe beyond a vague "ten to fifteen steps are involved" and "yes, chemicals are added to change the strength and the feel," the world's largest marshmallow is transformed into a dead ringer for fine, fashionable leather, good enough to become the swank, iconic Stella McCartney Falabella clutch bag with a chunky chain strap. (The bag was never for sale, but Stella, who is one of Jamie's closest business partners, made the purse as proof of concept and unveiled the masterpiece at a big London fashion shindig.)

Working with big-name partners is how Jamie plans to get this new leather to the masses. In 2020, she and the Bolt Threads team signed on with McCartney, Adidas, Lululemon, and Kering (which owns Gucci, Yves Saint Laurent, Bottega Veneta, and Balenciaga), and Bolt's first million square feet of leather is already promised to these companies.

One sticky issue is that the cow-leather industry is claiming that non-animal materials cannot be labeled true leather. "The same thing is happening with oat milk and Impossible burgers. You have to say 'oat drink.' The burger guys claim 'burger' means 'beef.' The dairy guys say milk comes from cows," Jamie explained. For now, Bolt calls its precious product Mylo, "the un-leather," the superior equivalent.

FACT: In 2012, Yale students found that mycelium in the Amazon rain forest can survive on a diet of only plastic. This mushroom root is able to break down polyurethane plastic on its own. They wonder if it can be used at the bottom of landfills to slowly break down plastics there.

VII

Food Fight

Jenny Du

Vice President of Operations at

Apeel Sciences

Doubling avocados' life span

I AM ODDLY GOOD AT: volleyball (particularly since I'm relatively short for the sport.)

I AM ODDLY BAD AT: Long-distance individual endurance sports. . . . I have a lot of respect for folks who can endure a high level of physical discomfort for extended periods.

MY GREATEST FEAR: disappointing others

A GUILTY PLEASURE: Hobnobs cookies. I'm addicted, so I can't have them in the house!

THE TRAIT I MOST DEPLORE IN MYSELF: desire for all things that I do to be perfect—totally unrealistic and consumes more energy than I should give it

AN OCCASION WHEN I LIE: to not have my parents worry about me

Is there anything more satisfying than guacamole on a salty tortilla chip? Avocado on toast? Avocado in a California roll? Is there anything more dispiriting than setting out to make guacamole, avocado toast, or California rolls and discovering all your three-dollar avocados are dark brown inside, rotten to the core?

> **FACT:** One in four avocados that reaches your kitchen gets tossed in the garbage.

> **FACT:** One in three avocados rots before it ever makes it into your cart.

> **FACT:** We are filling our landfills with pricey precious avocados.

Should you be bothered by these stats from the National Resources Defense Council (NRDC) based on data on all fruits and veggie waste? Is saving avocados going to save the planet? Probably not. But figuring out how to maintain an avocado's freshness may be the key to unlocking one of the mysteries of food preservation: How can we keep fruits and vegetables fresher longer? And answering that not-so-little question could very well cut methane emissions immensely, an essential step in the battle to save the planet.

Chemist Jenny Du felt she ought to try.

She remembers the day she first started down this very mushy rabbit hole, chasing the avocado holy grail. Her University of San Diego lab buddy James Rogers had just come back from a road trip to UC Berkeley that had taken him through the Salinas Valley, and he wanted to tell her all about the crops he'd seen out his window, how transfixed he'd been by the scale and magnitude of it all. Garlic and lettuce and artichokes as far as the eye could see. Mixed with his excitement was sadness, though, and

Jenny would soon learn why. He had recently learned the fact that nearly half the crops he'd driven by would rot before they reached any mouths, he told her.

On top of that, the crops that do make it to become food also frequently go bad before they are consumed, so this waste goes to landfill, where more troubling events happen. With all the stuffing and compressing and more stuffing of trash into landfills, every iota of oxygen gets squished out. Without oxygen, food can't decompose. So that overripe avocado quickly becomes a mini factory for methane—the heat-trapping gas that supercharges global warming. If that's not enough, that trashed avo, which never even became a happy snack, guzzled resources for months before reaching you—water, pesticides, power for refrigeration, diesel for transport. Waste on waste on waste.

The shame of how much food gets tossed stuck with Jenny like a bad nickname. Puzzles like "how to save half of all produce from rotting" were what Jenny and James lived for. By using the tools of their field—materials chemistry—Jenny was answering questions like "Can paint be used to capture the sun's rays for energy?" And "Is there a sensor that can detect microscopic metal in the air?" Through research and experimentation, Jenny and her lab partners were working on the paint and sensor posed by those queries. Now she wanted to take the same research-and-formulate approach to preserve food.

First, Jenny and James had to strip the main problem down to its component parts. Produce, they knew, goes bad for two main reasons: moisture seeps out, and oxygen seeps in. That's why that apple you left half-eaten on your car dash went brown where you chomped away the skin. No peel, no protection. So it's the peel or skin that protects the apple or avocado or cucumber or mandarin. But, apparently, not well enough. . . .

For weeks, Jenny and James brainstormed and researched. What might protect an avocado or an apple or a cucumber better and longer than their own skins?

Jenny is a meticulous researcher, according to James. She's creative but practical. Around the lab, she's known as the make-sh*t-happen girl. This time was no different. Her research took her all the way back to the origins of agriculture, when skins and peels first popped out of the ground a couple of billion years ago. Before that time, Earth was under water. Only a few islands poked above the surface. Plants were all submerged. With climate shifts, the oceans retreated, and land-based life emerged. Plants then had to withstand the elements. Skins and peels evolved to protect fruits and vegetables from harsh sun, high wind, pelting rain.

Around the lab, she's known as the make-sh*t-happen girl.

To enable himself and Jenny to dedicate substantial time to their exploration, James began writing a grant proposal. Scientists typically have to scrape together funding for the time and materials to chase new ideas. In the proposal, he described the problem, the goal, and experiments they'd like to conduct, and asked for financial support to go further. The 2012 grant proposal caught a big fish—the Bill & Melinda Gates Foundation. The husband-and-wife power duo (with their Microsoft billions) was always on the lookout for bold ideas to end world hunger. Bill and Melinda, who have since divorced, gave Jenny and James not only enough to continue researching. They gave them $100,000—enough to start a company.

Jenny and James dug in. They hit the supermarket to see up close the ingenious skins and peels Mother Nature had formed all those billions of years ago. The chemists brought home a pack of tomatoes and a bag of grapes and started fiddling. They boiled the skins, sometimes adding seeds or oils, to watch the reactions. Jenny scribbled observations and outcomes, and devised more experiments.

Here's what they figured out: Fruit and veggie skins and peels all contain similar building blocks. Fatty acids—also called lipids—link together to form an outer layer that locks in moisture. The denser the arrangement of lipids, the longer the produce can resist rot. Picture those Babybel cheeses with the red wax shells protecting the soft yellow disc inside. If James and Jenny's hypotheses were correct, in the lab they could create an extra layer of skin or peel—edible, of course, plus colorless, odorless, tasteless, and invisible to the shopper—that would at least double the life span of the fruit or vegetable it covered.

Apeel Sciences, the company name they picked, for obvious reasons, had a lot of work to do to jump from concept to creation. Back in the lab, Jenny went back to cooking peels of all kinds and breaking them down into their component parts. Sometimes she'd evaporate the liquid; other times she'd filter or strain her mixture. Her goal was to isolate the lipid material, then reduce the lipids to a concentrated powder, which could be added to water. This liquid would then get sprayed on at the packing plant, and maybe even someday in the fields, she thought.

Eventually the concoction was ready to test. She and James spritzed avocados. They coated apples, asparagus, limes, bananas. Later came mandarins, lemons, cucumbers. Then they set up cameras, zooming in on Apeel-coated produce on one side of a table and "naked" produce on the other. They programmed the camera to snap a pic every few hours, for a month.

The little time-lapse films revealed a miracle. By day four, the Apeel avocados remained vibrant green, while the non-treated ones had started darkening. By day nine, Apeel avocados looked as spiffy as on day four, while the naked 'cados were ready for Botox. By day twenty, the uncoated fruits looked burnt and shriveled, while the Apeel avocados were ready to top toast.

By day nine, Apeel avocados looked as spiffy as on day four, while the naked 'cados were ready for Botox.

Bill and Melinda Gates had bet on the right chemists.

Five years later, Jenny was standing outside the door of a packing plant listening to booming conveyor belts and workers applying her coating for extending the life of produce to huge quantities at one time. Business was booming. In 2018, Apeel introduced its coated avocados to several stores in the popular Midwest chain Kroger. Immediately, waste was cut in half. Soon after, Kroger rolled out Apeel avocados in eleven hundred of its stores. After that, Walmart came knocking. Yes, Walmart, where 25 percent of the country's fresh produce is sold.

Now nearing five hundred employees, with offices all over the world, Apeel has supplied Costco and big chains in Germany and Denmark. And, as planned, Apeel is reaching beyond avocados. In Washington State, the Apeel team is extending the life of apples, working with one of the state's largest organic growers. And, you know those extra-long English cucumbers with the ridiculous condom-esque plastic wrappers? In September 2020, Walmart ditched the plastic jacket and began offering Apeel-coated cukes instead.

There's something totally wacky about jackets for fruits and vegetables, but Jenny is far from wacky. It's the logic and rules and non-wackiness of chemistry that attracted her to the subject in the first place. "What seemed amorphous suddenly had this underlying order," she said, recalling her first brush with the science of substances.

Order is what you seek when your parents are both refugees, their outlook forged in the chaos of war. "We've been running away from Communism for a few generations," Jenny said of her family. Her parents eventually found jobs in Canada as blue-collar workers, welders mostly, and her dad's education topped out at sixth grade. It was the kind of childhood in which any activity that took Jenny away from studying was met with parental disapproval. Why would she risk her grades and all that academic achievement could bring in the way of opportunity for time with friends? they'd ask. She understood what they wanted of her, what they were trying to secure, but she refused to forget about her passion for spiking the volleyball. She tried out and made the high school team. She got a part-time job to pay her team expenses, and eventually played competitively in college. "That taught me to stick my neck out for things I really believed in," she said, even the fun stuff.

She really believes in Apeel. Jenny and crew have already kept twenty million pieces of produce from being dumped by retailers, lots of them avocados. In some instances, Apeel is tripling and quadrupling produce's edibility window. But the enormity of what she's attempting stresses her out sometimes. She doubts herself. She's used to being on top of every loose string, but starting a company, well, there's just so much around the corner that a person can't see. Those uncertainties keep her up at night. But, she's said, she'd rather be scared than bored: "Fear and excitement—that is the razor's edge you want to be walking along."

Starting in 1987, a University of Arizona professor named William Rathje and his students started opening up landfills, approaching the contents like archeologists on a dig. Over two decades, using a piece of heavy equipment called a bucket auger, they scooped vertical shafts out of twenty-one landfills, each one almost like a time capsule. The exercise was phase two of the Garbage Project, a thirty-year study begun in 1973 that used trash as a way to understand American culture and human behavior. What they found cutting into landfill is that food doesn't turn to dirt or dust—it mummifies. Because the landfills are so tightly packed that no oxygen can enter, food doesn't break down. So the team unearthed a forty-year-old pack of hot dogs—as good as new. A head of twenty-five-year-old lettuce looking plenty edible. They even found an order of guacamole next to a newspaper dated 1967, and it was barely brown.

Emily Stengel

Co-Executive Director and Cofounder of

GreenWave

Making kelp cool—to save the
oceans, farmers, and our food system

I AM ODDLY GOOD AT: remembering names

I AM ODDLY BAD AT: dancing (doesn't stop me)

MY GREATEST FEAR: losing my family/being buried alive/climate change

A GUILTY PLEASURE: gummy candy

I ADMIRE: Dr. Ayana Elizabeth Johnson, a marine biologist who talks about complex climate issues in a way that's real, relatable, and concrete—and lifts up other women along the way.

THE TRAIT I MOST DEPLORE IN MYSELF: self-criticism

AN OCCASION WHEN I LIE: when avoiding a social situation

MY GREATEST ACHIEVEMENT: NYC marathon

SOMETHING I USED TO DO BEFORE I REALIZED HOW BAD IT WAS FOR THE ENVIRONMENT: use plastic products with reckless abandon

Have you ever read an article that changed your life? Emily Stengel has. It was 2015, and she was lazing away a Sunday afternoon in Brooklyn with her latest *New Yorker,* when she got sucked into a story about kelp. The main character was a quirky Canadian named Bren Smith who quit high school to become a cod fisherman. When cod populations dwindled, he caught salmon, and when the salmon split for colder waters, he farmed oysters. Then two successive hurricanes buried his shellfish beds. So, kelp.

Kelp, Bren argued in the article, was Jack's magic beanstalk. The leaves grow three-quarters of an inch a day—no fertilizer, pesticides, or fresh water needed. Kelp absorbs carbon at five times the rate that land plants clean the air. It can even vacuum up pesticide-laden agricultural runoff that kills reefs. And farmers can grow it while they're doing other labor-intensive ocean-based projects, like farming mussels and clams, because it's dead easy. Kicker: mix kelp into animal feed, and cow farts are suddenly less lethal—that is, planet-warming emissions are massively reduced.

Kelp absorbs carbon at five times
the rate that land plants clean the air.

Emily, then twenty-nine years old, buried her nose deeper in the magazine.

Bren was starting what might be best termed the Great New England Kelp Movement. None of the slithery sea veggie's many benefits could be realized unless he could make kelp farming the Next Big Thing.

His overarching vision was to assist twenty-five locals in need of work—frustrated fishermen, unemployed military vets, low-on-luck land farmers—to start twenty-five small ocean farms near his home base in Connecticut. He was promoting what he called "sea basket" farming. Instead of fishing for one species of fish or shellfish per usual, leaving the harvester vulnerable to dwindling populations, hurricanes, and seasonal availability, he advocated a tidy mix starring kelp. Kelp easily and efficiently grows alongside clams, oysters, and scallops, all in his novel vertical design that occupies an entire narrow water column from surface to sea bottom.

If his approach to jump-starting the adoption of kelp farming worked in the Connecticut waters, he would copy this model elsewhere. The model works like this: GreenWave's hatchery incubates kelp seeds, plus baby mussels, clams, and oysters—all for distribution to farmers. The nonprofit then teaches new kelp farmers how to grow the kelp, what supplies to have on hand, how to design a plot—all intel available on an easy online platform. He would open a market to sell their wares (kelp smoothies would be served) and a processing facility right nearby because kelp spoils quickly after harvest so must be immediately processed. Former president Bill Clinton hailed the idea; the Buckminster Fuller Institute awarded Bren a $100,000 prize for an innovative solution to a global problem.

"Why isn't everyone doing this, right now?" Emily thought. And "I've got to meet this guy."

Emily had been a sustainable-food nut since before she'd had any idea what the word "sustainable" meant. As a girl, her favorite afternoons were spent picking wild strawberries and raspberries around Pennsylvania Amish country, where she grew up. Her first job, at twelve, was working a farm stand. After college, she joined a niche New York City catering company focused on local food. "It was very farm-to-table before that was cool," she said. Her gig after that was an investigation for the US Department of Agriculture into why the farm population was dwindling. (Lack of childcare weighs heavily, she learned.)

Emily found her way to Bren after some digging revealed they had a mutual friend. He invited her out to visit Thimble Island Ocean Farm, his plot in the Long Island Sound. She took the train to New Haven, where he was waiting in his bright orange truck. At his house, she plopped down at his dining table, and when she next glanced at her watch, eight hours had passed. They were already drawing organizational charts and workflow diagrams to grow the business.

Within days, it was set. They each had found the business partner they wanted. Together they would launch GreenWave, a nonprofit expansion of Bren's original idea. "He is the farmer, and I make everything happen," she said.

GreenWave essentially provides everything needed to get growing—an ocean farm-in-a-box is a way to think about the concept. All the ocean farmer wannabe needs is access to a boat, $30,000 to cover start-up costs like permits and materials, and a desire to become a kelp and shellfish farmer. Most of GreenWave's growers start with just one or two acres, with each acre able to produce 25 tons of greens and 250,000 shellfish per acre in five months. There is plenty of opportunity for expansion, and the output can get interesting, fast. A 20-acre farm can produce 130,000 pounds of kelp and 200,000 pounds of shellfish in a single year. You've probably heard the adage "Give a man a fish, he'll eat for a day; teach a man to fish, he'll eat for a lifetime." Emily built a business around it.

A kelp farm doesn't look like much from the ocean's surface. All you'd see if you floated by would be a bunch of red and white buoys bobbing about six feet apart. They hold a taut horizontal rope that anchors a vertical garden. Lantern-shaped nets hang down, holding thousands of M&M-sized scallops maturing to full size, and next to those hang "socks" full of maturing mussels. Then, on either side, ropes dangle, wrapped in fishing line coated in kelp seeds. A cluster of clam and oyster baskets sits on the ocean floor just beneath.

To harvest the crop, the grower uses a pulley system run off a boat to haul the ropes—loaded down with full-grown kelp—up onto the boat.

If a farmer follows GreenWave's instructions, she will grow a lot of kelp, and Emily will help sell that crop. The nonprofit even guarantees the purchase of 80 percent of its grower's harvest, at three times market rates, for five years. Talk about jump-starting an industry.

Who's buying? Well, it has taken some evangelizing, but Emily and Bren have shown restaurants and clever chefs what kelp can do on the plate. Sweet potato kelp flake soup and garlic sesame kelp salad. Oh my. Google is buying up kelp by the cartload for its employee cafeterias, because kelp is the new buzz-food. Emily gets that these are the buzz-makers, too, who will help this new food go mainstream. Kelp is being made into kelp spaghetti, kelp burgers, kelp jerky, kelp chips, kelp pickles. Kelp is being brewed into beer and dried into flour to make pasta. And you'll soon see

lots of nonedible kelp products, too: kelp laundry detergent, kelp bioplastics, kelp fertilizer, even kelp reusable diapers! It's that multipurpose.

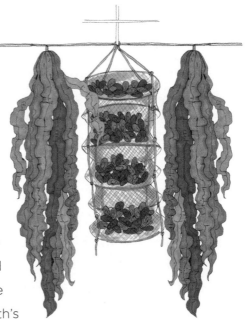

All well and good, but there's a bigger picture here. The really revolutionary idea they were building was a scalable model for all future agriculture. The ocean is ripe for picking up the food production slack that the earth's land can no longer handle. Agriculture sucks up three-quarters of the earth's fresh water and requires 40 percent of the land. The ocean, in contrast, covers 70 percent of the earth and now produces less than 2 percent of our food. The ocean is an untapped resource. "A network of small underwater farms totaling the size of Washington State could feed the entire planet," Emily's partner Bren touted on his blog. Best of all, farming kelp and other seaweed requires literally nothing but the seeds. No fresh water. Zippo fertilizer. "The footprint is negative," Emily often says.

A network of small underwater farms totaling the size of Washington State could feed the entire planet, Emily's partner Bren touted on his blog.

To fully appreciate what GreenWave is doing, one has to understand the dire state of our biggest bodies of water, too. Since the start of the Industrial Revolution, our oceans have been fighting global warming almost single-handedly, absorbing nearly 40 percent of carbon dioxide emissions, according to a Columbia University study published in *AGU Advances*. But the cracks are starting to show. Oceans are warming. Coral reefs are dying, which means the whole surrounding ecosystem withers.

Since the start of the Industrial Revolution, our oceans have been fighting global warming almost single-handedly, absorbing nearly 40 percent of carbon dioxide emissions.

Growing more kelp, moving farming off land and into the water, it shifts us back in the right direction. In GreenWave's first year, five farmers joined their in-person training. Today, GreenWave has supported the start of 195 farms and trained over 250 regenerative ocean farmers, and has a wait-list seven thousand people long, from a hundred countries. Their ten-year goal is ten thousand regenerative ocean farmers planting one million acres and yielding meaningful economic and climate impacts.

Many GreenWave farmers are women. And Native communities in Alaska and New Zealand—watching their centuries-old coastal existence erode with warming waters (causing disappearing fish) and rising seas—have found salvation in the farm techniques GreenWave is teaching.

Emily dreams of oceans teeming with lush underwater mini Edens. But there is nothing "mini" about a global kelp market set to hit $9 million by 2024.

> **FACT:** If ocean farmers devoted a little less than 5 percent of US waters to growing seaweed, they could clean up an estimated 135 million tons of carbon, a World Bank report found.

> **HINT:** Seaweed is a superfood. "Native seaweed contain more vitamin C than orange juice, more calcium than milk, and more protein than soybeans," Emily's partner, Bren Smith, says. More, the heart-healthy Omega-3 nutrients many seek out by eating fish are not created by the fish—"they consume them. By eating the plants fish eat, we get the same benefits while reducing pressure on fish stocks," he adds.

Kayla Abe

Cofounder of
Ugly Pickle Co.,
Shuggies Trash Pie,
and Natural Wine

Saving the misshapen, the oddballs,
the discolored—because they still taste delish

I AM ODDLY GOOD AT: finding great flight deals

I AM ODDLY BAD AT: roller-skating, memorizing numbers (can barely repeat a phone number back), recognizing actors between movies (lol)

MY GREATEST FEAR: I've become obsessed with eliminating fears. I've found all of mine (fear of writing, of running) to be irrational, and I try to eradicate them by turning them into my strengths (I'm nuts) by getting paid for my writing, and running a half marathon (check, check!).

A GUILTY PLEASURE: Thrifting! Antiquing! But not that guilty . . .

THE TRAIT I MOST DEPLORE IN MYSELF: always compromising my own needs for others

AN OCCASION WHEN I LIE: Ha, like a three-year-old, I guess I do feign ignorance when the last of the favorite foods disappear at home.

MY GREATEST ACHIEVEMENT: rock climbing the second-largest granite monolith in the world

> **FACT:** More than two-thirds of all food discarded in people's homes was potentially edible, a study by the NRDC conducted in Denver, Nashville, and New York found.

> **FACT:** Globally, 1.6 billion tons of produce are wasted a year, with a value of about a trillion dollars.

It's a race to see who will get to the carrot tops first—Kayla Abe's knife or wild rabbits. Rabbits have a natural advantage—their noses are highly tuned for carrots. But Kayla has a notebook full of phone numbers of family farmers who love her.

On any given Saturday morning, you can find her at the San Francisco Ferry Plaza Farmers Market under a banner of green felt letters that spell out "EAT UGLY." She made and strung the sign herself—all part of her vegetable-whisperer persona.

"Do you like spicy?" she sings out to passersby, holding up her colorfully labeled jar of Spicy Bread 'N' Buttah pickles. If she gets a smile, she continues—"Everything inside is 'upcycled'!"

Upcycled pickles? Yes. In 2016, she and her boyfriend/sidekick David Murphy founded Ugly Pickle Co., an indie brand of condiments, pickles, and spreads made from rejected produce—limp three-legged carrots, sun-spotted cukes, bruised apples, etc. Not even soup kitchens want some of these castoffs, even when they're plenty delicious. (Hot tip: limp carrots have higher than normal sugar content and are particularly flavorful roasted up.) So, Kayla and David pay small family farmers for fruits and veggies spurned by beauty-conscious consumers and turn them into edible Cinderellas.

They even work with parts of fruits and vegetables that were never intended for retail, like cauliflower leaves, and the aforementioned carrot tops. These "rescue" efforts are particularly thrifty, because Ugly Pickle Co. is generating income from items that would typically have no market.

Kayla and David's business came together soon after the couple met in 2014 at San Francisco's primo farm market, where they now have their stand. He was a San Francisco chef purchasing melons and wax beans for a restaurant called Whitechapel (a gin bar known for great food, not the food chain). She was working for the nonprofit that manages the farmers' market. A bit of banter over the spiciness of the arugula led to Kayla visiting David's restaurant. Not thirty seconds into that second meeting, they shared an accidental wet kiss. (He went in for a French-style two-cheek greeting. She wasn't expecting it, so when she turned her head, his lips landed on hers, and . . .) Now they live, cook, invent, and work together. Sometimes they even wear matching pickle necklaces and Hawaiian pickle shirts.

Kayla was peeved about food waste long before she met David. While at Vassar College, she helped create a food sustainability master plan for her campus. Next, she went to work for the Center for Urban Education About Sustainable Agriculture, which promotes sustainable agriculture and runs the San Francisco Ferry Plaza Farmers Market. After that, she went to work as a market development manager for Oatly, that addictive oat-milk product that's lowering methane output by providing an alternative to dairy. She's still with Oatly, making the steady income that's allowing them to grow their new enterprises.

Before Kayla started Ugly Pickle or even worked at the San Francisco

Ferry Plaza Farmers Market, she was a farmers' market groupie. She'd watch trucks unload in the morning and reload at the end of the day, sometimes with just as much produce as they'd come with. A farmer's life is like that. The weather goes suddenly south, so no one shows up with their canvas totes to shop the stalls. Small growers rarely have extensive refrigeration, so their plump stone fruit and fast-to-wilt basil quickly turns to mush, and becomes unsalable within a few days. Food wasted. David saw the other side of it at the restaurant. He'd be expecting two cases of cucumbers to arrive at his kitchen, but six would show up. Why? Because the farmer hadn't planned on a heat wave making all his cucumbers ripen at once. Well, David wasn't going to turn the food away. He knew that sometimes excess produce is left to rot in the field when farmers realize that picking and trucking to market will actually lose them money. Better to buy the cukes and find some use for them.

Kayla and David determined, based on the anecdotal evidence and extensive research out there, that food waste is a massive problem. Food that gets tossed could feed an additional two billion people around the globe, University of Vermont and Department of Agriculture researchers reported in 2018. Fruits and vegetables, plus roots and tubers, have the highest wastage rates of any food. About twenty billion pounds of food waste comes from farms that can't find buyers for their produce, the *New Republic* reported. Meanwhile, hunger is so pervasive in America that millions of college students are "food insecure." Even if just one-fourth of the food currently lost or wasted globally could be saved, it would be enough to feed 870 million hungry people in the world, the United Nations Environment Program reports. How insane is this? Hunger is largely a logistical problem. Try telling that to someone who hasn't eaten in two days. (Remember Komal Ahmad's World's Dumbest Problem?)

*Food that gets tossed could feed an
additional two billion people around the globe.*

Kayla loves what she's doing, but it's hard. Each day is a combination of expletives, do-overs, and screw-ups. Examples: (1) Upon seeing the Ugly labels for the first time, perusers equated "food waste" with "dumpster diving," and walked away. ("Food waste" was later removed from labels.) (2) A trip to buy two thousand pickle jars ended with boxes flying open and glass jars flying out and shattering on the highway as Kayla drove home.

Being a small company also means getting snubbed by suppliers, delivery outfits, and shipping companies. It means there's a lot of DIY to the whole operation. When three giant pallets of ugly cucumbers come off the farm, either Kayla or David has to drive to Los Angeles, rent a U-Haul, and pick them up. Every couple of weeks. Then they personally escort their oddball cucumbers to their co-manufacturer in Santa Barbara. And when their stick-shift car stalls out and the pickles need to get to the market, they get out at the bottoms of hills and push.

Whenever Kayla gets discouraged, she thinks of her paternal grandfather who farmed for decades in the Salinas Valley. Like so many other small farmers, he was up against giant corporate competitors, inclement weather, fluctuating prices. Today she is helping farmers like him stay afloat and preserving loads of food in the process.

Her efforts are paying off. In 2021, Whole Foods—the mother of all accounts—began selling Ugly pickles. And the same year, she and David opened a pizza place called Shuggies Trash Pies in the Mission neighborhood of San Francisco. Why pizza? It offers a blank canvas on which to throw all variety of reject produce. "Not everyone likes pickles," David said, "but everyone likes pizza."

Funding from the Crowd: Lots of Tiny Donations = Big Money

Every year in North America, $17 billion is raised via crowdfunding to fund projects from Soapbottle, where the container itself is soap, to the Click and Grow 25, a mini indoor "farm." The approach lets you tap friends, acquaintances, and complete strangers. Pitching to venture capitalists and foundations for money works well for über-connected people, but crowdfunding can happen with zero highbrow contacts. Kayla raised $58,213 on Kickstarter toward her new pizza restaurant.

Here are some crowdfunding basics, and tips for raising the big bucks:

1. You must be eighteen years old to run a Kickstarter campaign. You can hack this by getting an adult to "sponsor" you and use their account. GoFundMe allows you to raise funds starting at age thirteen, with parental permission.

2. Give your campaign an easy-to-understand title such as "World's First Cardboard Furniture Co." or "Save Bozeman's Great Gray Owls." There are over twenty-six thousand environment-related campaigns on GoFundMe, so be creative with your communications to differentiate yours.

3. Create a short explanatory marketing video (the phone video cam works fine) to "sell" your idea, with a clear call to action.

Surprising statistics draw people in—for example, "Did you know that one-third of all US farmland is used to grow burgers?" If you can't make a video, use high-quality photos. You are appealing to emotions, so use images that create feeling. Share why this issue matters to you personally, because that is what creates motivation and urgency among donors.

4. Set a fundraising goal. Be bold with your target, because this shows confidence in your idea. On both Kickstarter and Go-FundMe, you get whatever funds you raise even if you fail to hit your goal, so nothing is lost by aiming high.

5. Write a clear and compelling "ask." Avoid thick blocks of text. Instead use sections with headlines like "The Backstory," "The Costs," "Why I'm So Motivated," and "How You Can Help." Post pictures throughout to keep people reading.

6. Market the heck out of your campaign. If nobody sees your page, they can't donate. Share the link widely, even with people who are just acquaintances. Post a blurb and the link on Facebook, and add an end note like "Please help me by sharing with your network."

7. Campaign off-line as well as online. Try teaming up with a local pizza joint, because businesses love supporting causes that their consumers care about (makes the business look good, too); asking a local café to dedicate a menu item to your campaign, where sales for a week go to you; approaching your local book-store and pitching a partnership where a percentage of event sales go to your GoFundMe. In exchange, you'll bring all your friends by.

Now What?

Your head should be spinning. You have seen the future. These women are the change. Humanity is teetering, the time bomb is ticking, and here, finally, is hope! Possibility! Invention on overdrive! Enough cleverness and smart science to fill a big, fat book.

But that still leaves you at "Yes, sign me up, but where do I leap?" Which organization? Warming oceans or air? Electric cars or transportation policy? Does my thrift shopping matter a whiff when Big Oil is sinking us? You are set to join the fight of your lifetime, but figuring out the right move to make—paralyzing.

Remember that advice Sarah Paiji Yoo of Blueland always got from her dad? A bit corny, yes. But apropos. "You know how you eat an elephant?" he'd ask. The answer, of course, is "One bite at a time." Internalize this idea.

But agreed—even just finding the fork is intimidating.

The best path in is through your emotions. Notice what fires you up, what you are still heated or intrigued or obsessed about the next day, what you yearn to learn more about. It makes no difference how big or minuscule the idea is that struck you. Maybe you're grabbed by Cathy Zoi at EVgo opening hundreds of electric-car charging stations, and you want to join the transition to e-vehicles, or you are suddenly an Ecosia search engine addict, because you learned that they plant a tree for every search made. Maybe you're enchanted with Birch Run High School near Saginaw, Michigan, now running their buses off of leftover cafeteria French fry oil that students turn into biodiesel.

Note what cuts through the noise for you, what elicits feeling. Go there. Research that organization, write to those teens, apply for that internship. Did one of these thirty-four women make you wish you could work with them? Maybe you are motivated to gather signatures for Greenpeace's petition "Tell President Biden: Ban New Oil and Gas Permits," or you're marveling over Mary Anne Hitt shutting down 393 coal plants and want to help shutter the final 191. Don't overthink the decision of where to start. Go with your heart. That's when you'll find yourself wading in deeper and deeper.

Brilliant marine biologist, ocean activist, and *How to Save a Planet* podcast (which you must listen to, BTW) creator Ayana Elizabeth Johnson says that "I want to help. What should I do?" is the number one question she gets asked. She says grab a pad and draw a Venn diagram. Fill the first circle with whatever topic spurs real emotion. Your superpower goes in the second circle—yes, everyone has one. Are you a social media whiz like Leah Thomas? In your friend group, do you inevitably end up in charge, an organizer type like Varshini Prakash at Sunrise? Is tinkering and inventing your specialty, like the duos at Huue and Lillian Augusta? Maybe you're an artist or make films like Annie Leonard, or can code apps. That area of overlap between your passion and your power is your sweet spot. Try this, and see what emerges.

Remind yourself, too, that nearly all the eco-queens profiled here knew nothing, nada, zilch when they started out, and now they rule their realm. Gregg Renfrew—who helped pass two California bills upping cosmetics safety, and got more than eighteen thousand nasty chemicals out of the beauty products she sells by the millions—knew "nothing about beauty, nothing about direct selling, nothing about nothing," as she put it. These women built their enterprises with trial and error, thick skin, and very hard work. Most started with Googling, some with LinkedIn searches, or with mining their school's alumni directory.

Greenpeace USA head Annie Leonard says quit trying to be an eco-perfect person. Transfer that energy to actions that move the needle.

Build your "activist muscle," she says. Her point is that toting canvas bags to the grocery will only ever make an infinitesimal difference. Climate change is here, and we need policy overhauls, government regulations, big bold actions, which require organizing, lobbying, pressure campaigns, and voting in the right politicians. That last one is really key. Go to work on campaigns where climate champions are running; even town and state races really matter because consequential decisions happen at every level of government.

Starting locally is smart. You can't just go out and launch an effective protest against the Enbridge Line 3 pipeline. But if you know your stuff, likely your school would let you lead an assembly about the latest pipeline war. Then ask your audience to consider writing politicians in Minnesota, asking why these politicians think fifty coal plants' worth of new emissions is okay. If that works, make a video about what's happening with Line 3, and ask viewers to tweet @Enbridge, "Seriously, fifty coal plants' worth of greenhouse gases into a fast-heating atmosphere?" These starter actions sharpen your skills, which will allow you to take bigger actions, like using social media to amplify messages, persuading others to lend their voices, and using shocking statistics for impact.

Remember how many Get Out the Vote postcards were sent during the 2020 election? The post office literally ran out of stamps. A few hundred postcards rarely matter. But when over a billion more get sent than in the prior election, from all fifty states, they increase turnout. Each sender did, say, two hundred, but they roped in a friend, who then threw two postcard parties. . . . So, you see how this works.

Here's a revelation for you, and it's a doozy: You have a power of persuasion that I bet you don't even know about.

In 2019, academics at North Carolina State University wanted to figure out how to get adults who are skeptical or ill-informed about climate change to care more. They decided to run an experiment, because they had an instinct that kids' opinions and knowledge would flow to parents, the way so much knowledge flows from parents to kids. They taught climate science to two hundred or so kids over two years and tracked their parents' attitudes.

Turns out, having a climate-change-savvy tween or teen girl in the house is the best way to grow an army of climate activists. Teen girls change hearts and minds like nobody else. They are more persuasive than the boys—the researchers posit that perhaps it's because they are better communicators. Girl influence is real.

So start talking up these women's ideas. Talk about how kelp can kill the methane in cow farts so that less carbon dioxide gets trapped in the atmosphere, and talk about how solar mini-grids can produce energy. You can change mindsets, inspire, and grow the movement, starting in your own kitchen.

Work for companies and organizations that are on the right side of the climate fight. There are tons of published lists of the most sustainable companies in America. If the real talent won't work for the companies in denial, guess how fast their practices will start changing? And don't give the laggards/feet-draggers your business either. Stop spending money at the notorious fast-fashion retailers. Do your homework so you can ID the worst culprits.

Quitting fossil fuels is everything right now. So, march for that. Write postcards for that. Make phone calls for that. Work to elect politicians who are moving on that.

Your change-agent story starts now. Right now.

INFOGRAPHIC SOURCES

FOSSIL FUEL

1. National Geographic: nationalgeographic.com/environment/article/fossil -fuels
2. Ourworldindata.org: https://ourworldindata.org/fossil-fuels
3. CleanTechnica: https://cleantechnica.com/2019/04/01/claims-big-oil -invested-over-1-billion-on-misleading-climate-lobbying-since-paris -labelled-fanciful/
4. EndCoal.org: https://endcoal.org/climate-change/

CARS

1. Ford Corporate: https://corporate.ford.com/articles/history/the-model-t.html
2. Environmental Protection Agency: epa.gov/greenvehicles/fast-facts -transportation-greenhouse-gas-emissions
3. World Economic Forum: weforum.org/agenda/2016/04/the-number-of -cars-worldwide-is-set-to-double-by-2040
4. Policy Advice: https://policyadvice.net/insurance/insights/how-much-do -americans-drive/
5. *The New York Times:* nytimes.com/interactive/2021/03/10/climate/electric -vehicle-fleet-turnover.html
6. Federal Highway Administration: fhwa.dot.gov/ohim/summary95/mv200.pdf
7. Statista: https://www.statista.com/statistics/183505/number-of-vehicles-in -the-united-states-since-1990/

PLASTIC

1. Audubon Magazine: audubon.org/news/microplastics-are-literally-raining -our-national-parks-and-wilderness-areas
2. *The New York Times:* nytimes.com/1975/06/04/archives/cocacola-trying -a-plastic-bottle-pepsicola-contends-it-will.html
3. World Economic Forum Report: weforum.org/docs/WEF_The_New _Plastics_Economy.pdf
4. *The Guardian:* theguardian.com/business/2019/mar/14/coca-cola-admits -it-produces-3m-tonnes-of-plastic-packaging-a-year
5. UNEP (United Nations Environment): unep.org/interactive/beat-plastic -pollution/
6. Greenpeace: greenpeace.org/international/story/7281/every-single-piece -of-plastic-ever-made-still-exists-heres-the-story/
7. darrinqualman.com/global-plastics-production/
8. ourworldindata.org: https://ourworldindata.org/plastic-pollution

FAST FASHION

1. UNEP: unep.org/science-data
2. Ocean Clean Wash: oceancleanwash.org/science/
3. *Environmental Health:* https://ehjournal.biomedcentral.com/articles/10.1186 /s12940-018-0433-7
4. Council for Textile Recycling: weardonaterecycle.org
5. Harvard Business School using data from *Bloomberg/Business Week:* https://digital.hbs.edu/platform-digit/submission/zara-achieving-the-fast -in-fast-fashion-through-analytics/
6. Ellen MacArthur Foundation: ellenmacarthurfoundation.org/assets /downloads/A-New-Textiles-Economy_Full-Report_Updated_1-12-17.pdf
7. *Forbes:* forbes.com/sites/jamesconca/2015/12/03/making-climate -change-fashionable-the-garment-industry-takes-on-global-warming /?sh=fc7bc0779e41

MEAT

1. Sentient Media: https://sentientmedia.org/how-does-agriculture-cause-deforestation/
2. Visual Capitalist citing Poore & Nemecek (2018): visualcapitalist.com/visualising-the-greenhouse-gas-impact-of-each-food/
3. *Smithsonian Magazine:* smithsonianmag.com/science-nature/beef-uses-ten-times-more-resources-poultry-dairy-eggs-pork-180952103/
4. Institute for Agriculture and Trade Policy (IATP): https://grain.org/en/category/539-climate
5. USDA: https://apps.fas.usda.gov/psdonline/circulars/livestock_poultry.pdf

POPULATION GROWTH

1. theworldcounts.org
2. Our World in Data: https://ourworldindata.org/uploads/2013/05/WorldPopulationAnnual12000years_interpolated_HYDEandUNto2015.csv

CO$_2$ EMISSIONS

1. Climate Change News: climatechangenews.com/2016/09/02/the-woman-who-identified-the-greenhouse-effect-years-before-tyndall/
2. UNEP: https://unfccc.int/news/cut-global-emissions-by-76-percent-every-year-for-next-decade-to-meet-15degc-paris-target-un-report
3. Holmberg, Kenneth, and Ali Erdemir, "Influence of tribology on global energy consumption, costs and emissions," *Friction* 5 (2017): 263–84. https://link.springer.com/article/10.1007/s40544-017-0183-5
4. NASA: https://climate.nasa.gov/vital-signs/carbon-dioxide/
5. *Popular Science:* popsci.com/record-breaking-co2-graph-climate/

ACKNOWLEDGMENTS

I am awed by each of you thirty-four women profiled. Thank you for giving me precious time in your insanely busy lives and a window into the environmental revolution that I knew little to nothing about. Many of you also generously introduced me to your heroes, some of whom are now included as well.

Up top, I need to thank Danielle Svetcov, my gem of a talented, ever-encouraging agent, who wields a hell of an editing pen. I am so lucky to have had a coffee with you so many years ago on a Noe Valley corner (you wore one of your trademark hats). Thank you, Ana Jarén, for bringing these colorful, fabulous women to the pages looking as colorful and fabulous as they truly are. Appreciation to Andrea Lau and Regina Flath, my tasteful Delacorte design team. Beverly Horowitz at Delacorte Press, thank you for believing in me and jumping in to right things when I've needed you to. My editor, Alison Romig, I so value your enthusiasm for this project and your attentiveness. You are a great partner to me.

Elliot Singer, I love you for being so tough on my writing and scribbling "cringe" next to the many words and phrases where I had gone astray. You have saved me from myself. I am grateful to Robin Donohoe for brainstorming women to include early on, for sharing thoughts while hiking (so many of which you'll notice in my conclusion), and for making introductions to several tremendous entrepreneurs in your DRK Foundation portfolio.

I bow to Laura Debole for producing a beautiful proposal, weighing in on illustrators, and being my go-to "visual" consultant.

Caroline Paul, thanks for reading pages, suggesting women, and being a useful sounding board, always.

My daughter Emma, you inspired this book with your immediate reaching over to turn off the running water I waste while doing dishes inefficiently. You have been a great help, letting me bounce ideas, reacting to drafts and illustrations, and cheerleading me daily. My sister, Lisa, you always have the smartest feedback. When I needed someone to check my climate science but I couldn't bear to reveal to just anyone some of the simplest facts I am foggy on (that I should have learned back in high school), Dan Robison, you saved my bacon. Then you quickly connected me with Allison Crimmins, a climate scientist at the EPA, and she wrestled with many sentences and paragraphs, making sure How We Got Here was actually How We Got Here. Many kudos, Allison! You went way above and beyond. Brilliant Bree Sanchez, you took my mess of ideas and produced this gorgeous opening spread. Anne Marie Bourgoyne, thank you for connecting me to some of the biggest stars of this book.

My son, Kapp, much gratitude for your interest in my journalism, your forwarding of choice articles, your warnings about falling into the trap of greenwashing, and your continual challenging of my thinking about sustainability, which has made a difference all over this manuscript.

So many have weighed in with ideas about who and what to include and have made key connections, so thank you, Rafi Donohoe, Lily Kanter, Tina Sharkey, Cathy Zoi, Jesse Genet, Felicia Wong, Billy Funderburk, Chris Maxey, Sue Levin, Anne Loucks, Lisi Dean, and Amy Banse. My friends who listen and listen and listen, I wouldn't survive without you, Leela, Heidi, Tricia, Diane, Tia, Amy, Aimee, Rebecca, Hadley, Susie, and others I've surely forgotten.

Jim Lesser, you are a true creative, and I am the luckiest to tap your talents for free.

Blanca Sabillon, I so appreciate your taking care of everything and of me, too.

Rodes, I have written this whole book with you snapping your gum on the other side of the wall and occasionally in the leather therapy chair. Your humor and storytelling sustain me.

Oh, of course, my EMC, you continue to be the scaffolding my life hangs on.

Finally, David, the best wordsmith, the one who always knows everything and never stops giving.

ABOUT THE AUTHOR

Diana Kapp is a business journalist with an MBA from Stanford University who has written about education and entrepreneurism for most of the major media outlets. *Girls Who Run the World* was her first book.

dianakapp.com